This is not a wall

THIS IS NOT A WALL

Collected Short Stories on CODA'S *Party Wall* at MoMA PS1

O'Donnell, Chodoriwsky, editors

2017

Contents

I The Competition

II The Design Development

III The Install

IV The Wall

I

The Competition

Dear Caroline,

Kent Kleinman

I write to nominate you for the 2013 PS1 Young Architects Program (YAP), jointly sponsored by MoMA PS1 and The Museum of Modern Art. As a nominator for YAP, it is my pleasure to recommend you for the pool from which the program's jury will select the finalists for the 2013 installment of the program.

The finalists of YAP are asked to submit a design proposal for an environmentally friendly urban landscape for MoMA PS1's large entrance courtyard, made up of three outdoor spaces. The project aims to explore and improve upon the quality of public space by providing elements of shade, water, and seating—and also to focus on themes of sustainability, recycling, and reuse. The courtyard will be used both by visitors on the weekdays and by large numbers of young people during the Warm Up music series on Saturdays throughout the summer of 2013.

To be considered you must prepare and submit a portfolio with three relevant projects, a one-page statement, and a resume, in both print and PDF format, by November 5, 2012. Portfolios and statements will be reviewed by a group of MoMA and MoMA PS1 jurors in November 2012. This group will make a selection of five finalists who will be asked to submit a proposal at the day of the jury. The jury will interview the five candidates and make a final selection by mid-January 2013.

All materials must be submitted to the Department of Architecture and Design of the Museum of Modern Art, attention Emma Presler, emma_presler@moma.org.

Please let me know as soon as possible if you wish to participate in the program.

Sincerely,

Local loops, interrupted...

CODA

CODA is founded on the belief that sustainable solutions begin with attention to site: both the physical, spatial realities of site, but also, and more importantly, the invisible energy flows of sun, wind, water, local material sources, and energy flows. We produce work that is reactive to its context, and in which that reactiveness is legible.

CODA sniffs out the opportunities in the locale that can be hooked into and drawn out. This double approach—between sustainability and meaningful form—pervades all of our projects: *Bloodline: Self-Consuming Grill Pavilion* consumes its own skin through use as the architecture itself is recycled; *Urban Punc.* is a housing project that proposes no housing: instead we propose to maintain and reuse the existing housing stock, but insert infrastructural components in to gaps in the city fabric to reactivate and rehabilitate the existing city; *Tweak: Living Room* researches stimuli of fear in the public spaces of Spangen, Rotterdam, and proposes an installation that aims to reprogram the stereotypes of public spaces.

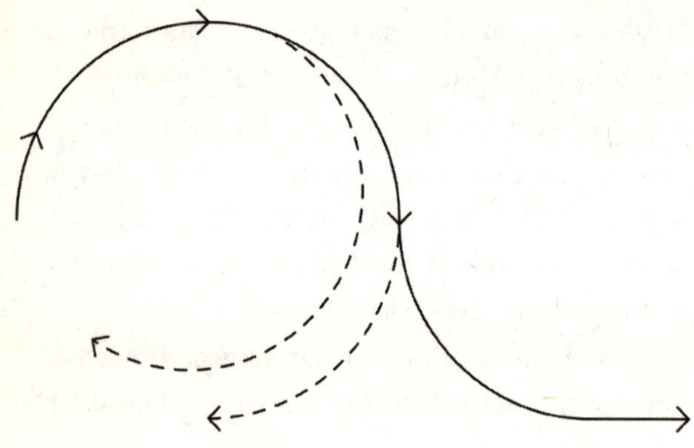

Skin (standard)

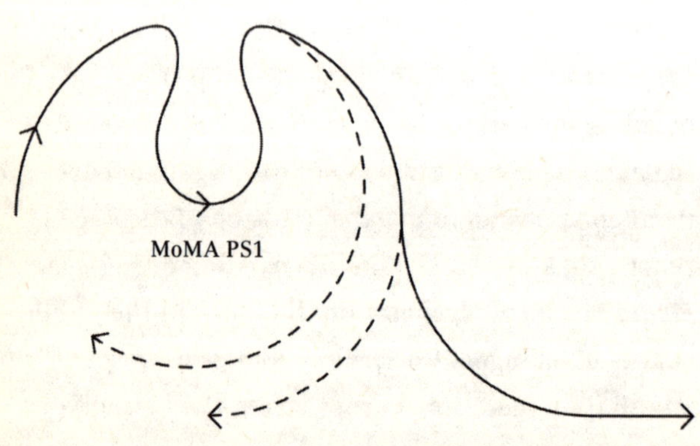

Skin (interrupted)

At PS1, CODA's approach will begin by understanding material and energy flows in the New York area and consider logistics of recycling already in place locally. Recycling factories compress aluminum in its various forms into like-sized "bales," which are stacked on warehouse floors awaiting their smelting. These cubes, identical in outline, differ in content: (the can, the strip, the coil, etc.) resulting in different densities and porosities. The cubes are gleaming and monolithic gabions. By borrowing these ready-made building blocks from their warehouses across New York City, the building materials only need to be transported a short distance to site. The design work then begins in mapping light qualities and directions to the space of PS1's courtyard to create pockets of spaces and landscapes that are choreographed with the place. The Baling Wall intervention will engage in the life cycle of an object of consumption, borrowing it from its cycle and returning it unconsumed. The public's engagement with the in-process aluminum raises the profile of aluminum's life-story (and aluminum has many lives).

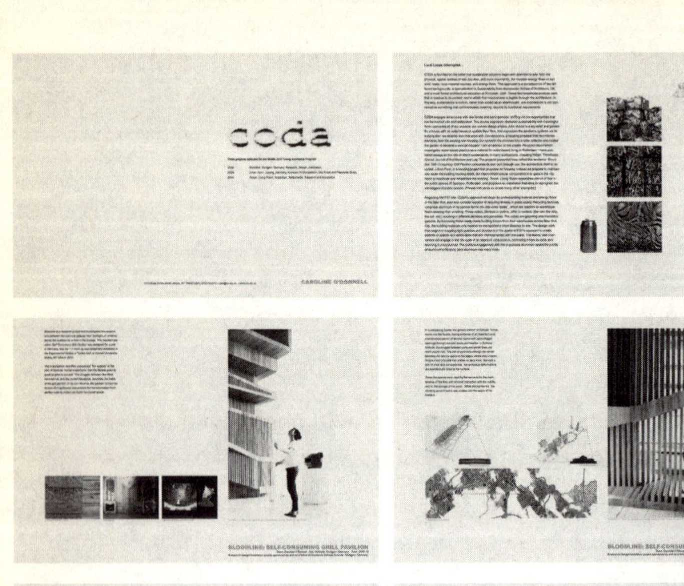
coda
CAROLINE O'DONNELL
STATEMENT
BLOODLINE: SELF-CONSUMING GRILL PAVILION
BLOODLINE: SELF-CONSUMING GRILL PAVILION

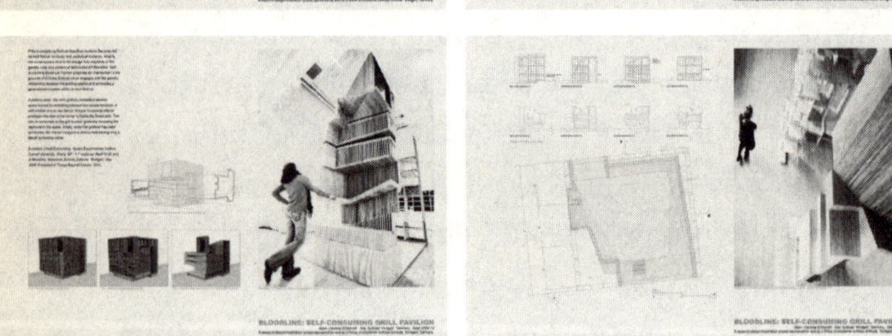
BLOODLINE: SELF-CONSUMING GRILL PAVILION
BLOODLINE: SELF-CONSUMING GRILL PAVILION

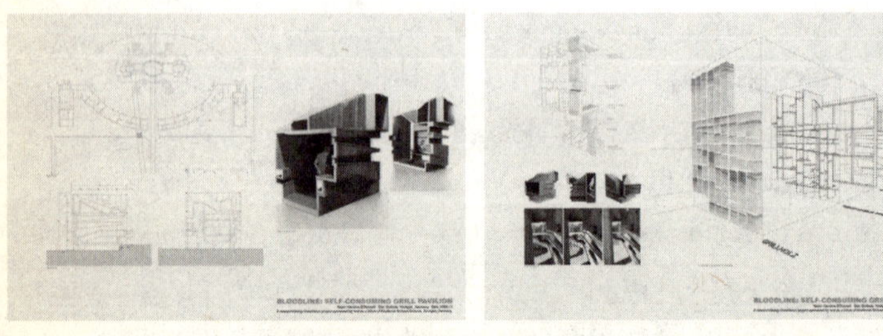
BLOODLINE: SELF-CONSUMING GRILL PAVILION
BLOODLINE: SELF-CONSUMING GRILL PAVILION

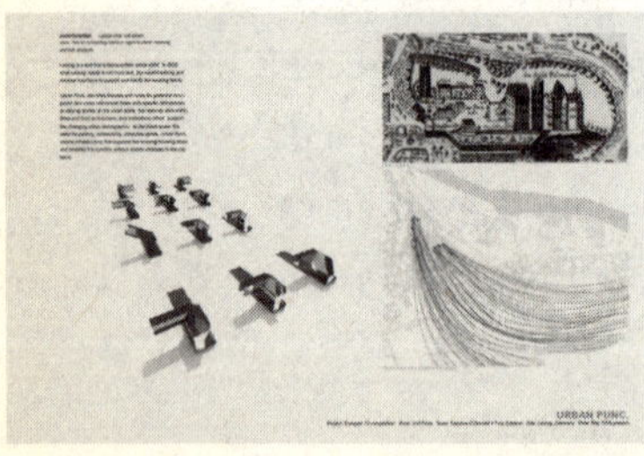
URBAN PUNC.

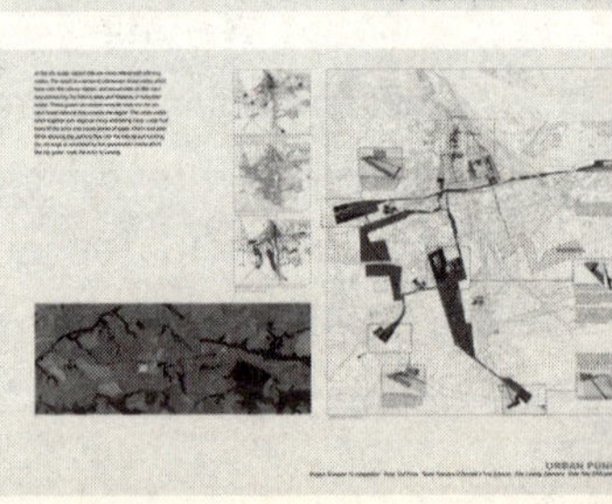
URBAN PUNC.

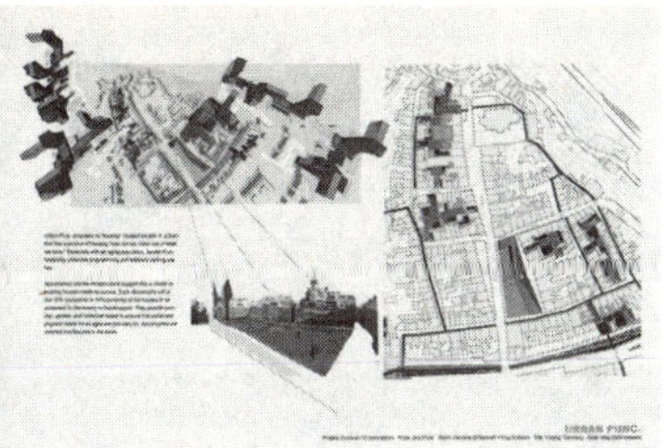
URBAN FUNC.

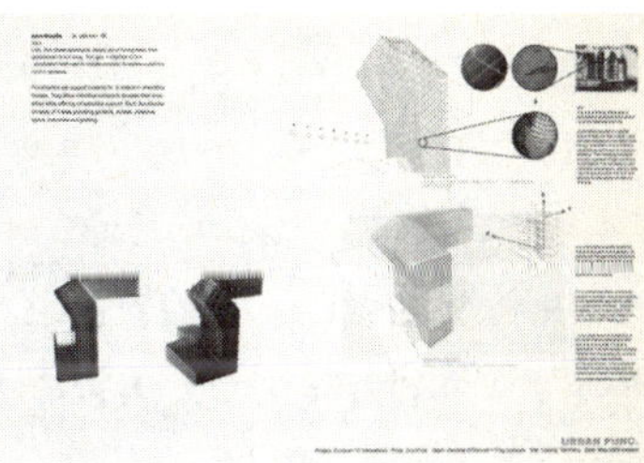
URBAN FUNC.

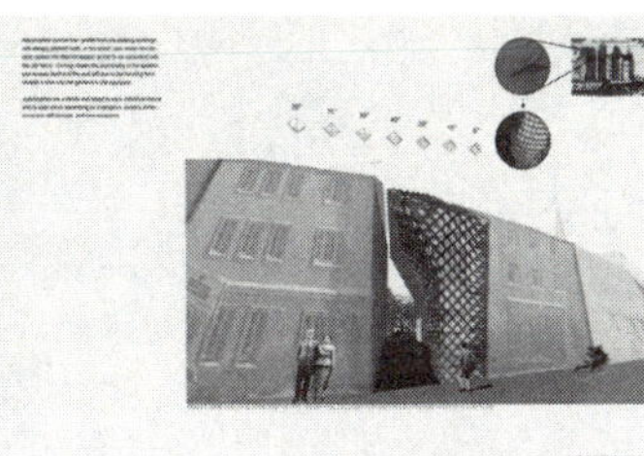

URBAN FUNC.

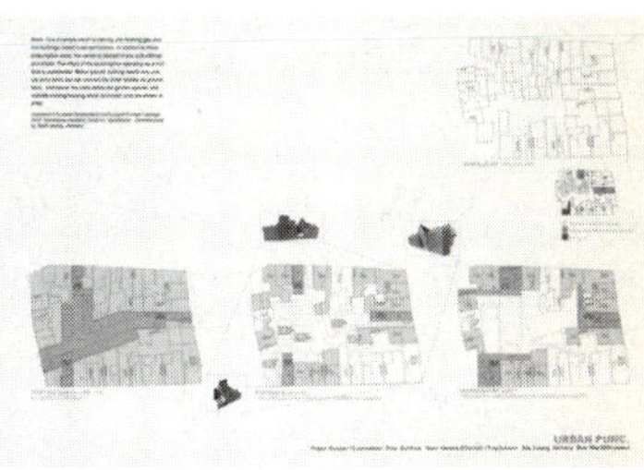
URBAN FUNC.

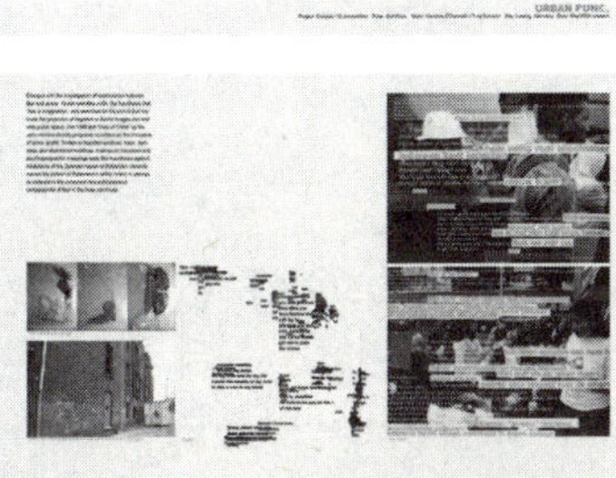

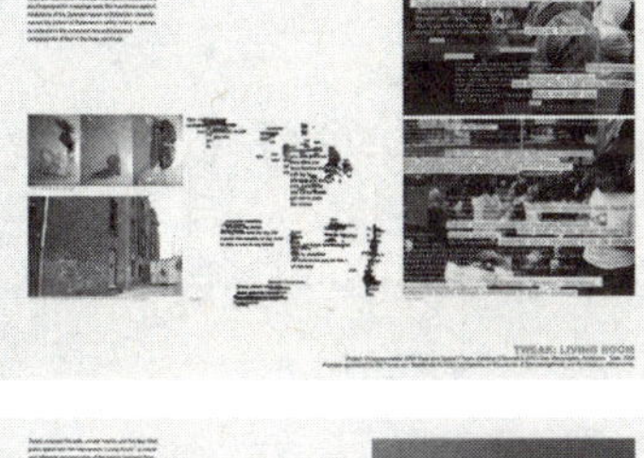
TWEAK: LIVING ROOM

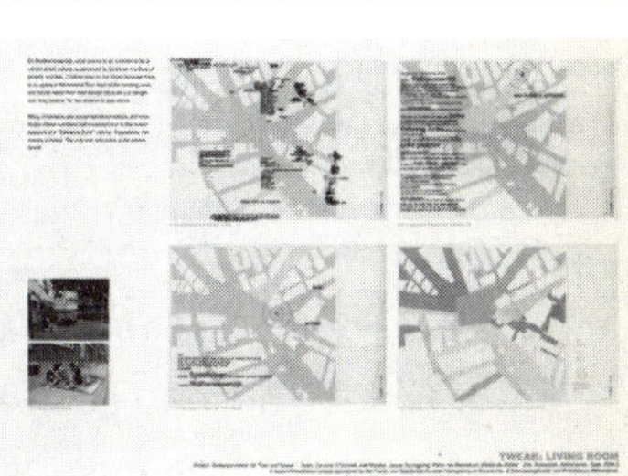
TWEAK: LIVING ROOM

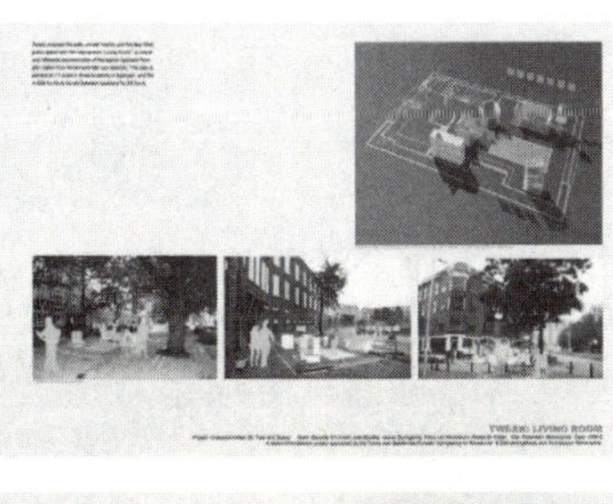
TWEAK: LIVING ROOM

TWEAK: LIVING ROOM

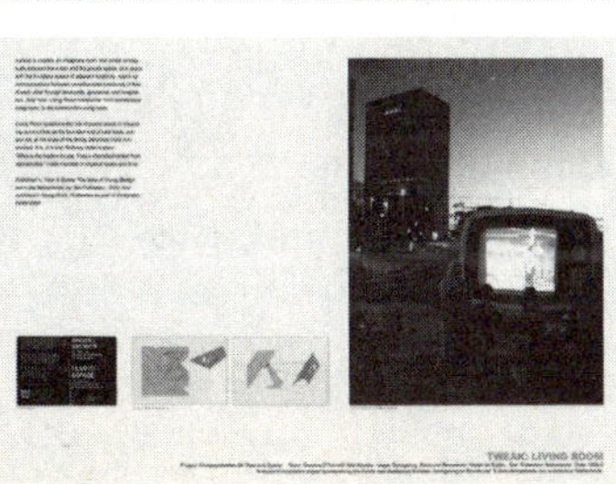
TWEAK: LIVING ROOM

coda
For more information and to see other work, please visit www.co-da.co

They want to throw an epic party

William O'Brien Jr.

On Sun, Nov 18, 2012 at 9:24 AM,
William O'Brien Jr. <wojr@mit.edu> *wrote:*

Re: Shortlisted!

Hi Caroline [22],

I'm so happy to see your name on the list of five finalists for PS1 this year. Just wanted to say best of luck—I hope to see you come out on top. Having competed in the past, I suppose the two things that I might relay are:

(1)

I found that the more cerebral aspects of a project don't gain as much traction with the MoMA PS1 jury as I would have hoped. I saw that the jury was very receptive to any aspects of the proposal that would "appeal to the masses" so some of the more nuanced, disciplinarily-focused arguments that were made were... not so relevant.

(2)

Panache and a bit of flamboyance go a long way. I opted for the stoic, more sculptural approach, with the party scene being considered a distant second... big mistake. Really, they want to throw an epic party for New York and they want the architectural proposal to be conducive to that. My recommendation would be to not take yourself so seriously as I did. Have fun with it. Good luck!

Very best,
Liam

In faux-fur booties

Caroline O'Donnell

Cold in the basement. I can see my breath. Cayuga Lake through the windows. I am wearing two layers of everything and the tatty purple faux-fur booties that my mother [47] gave me years ago. You need good slippers in America, nice warm feet. I should sit up near the stove, wait until the team is in place, relax. But we are in the final five. I have to do something.

Printed plan beneath trace, hazy under the vellum. Messy layout, triangular courtyard with a triangular penetration by the neighbor. I trace a

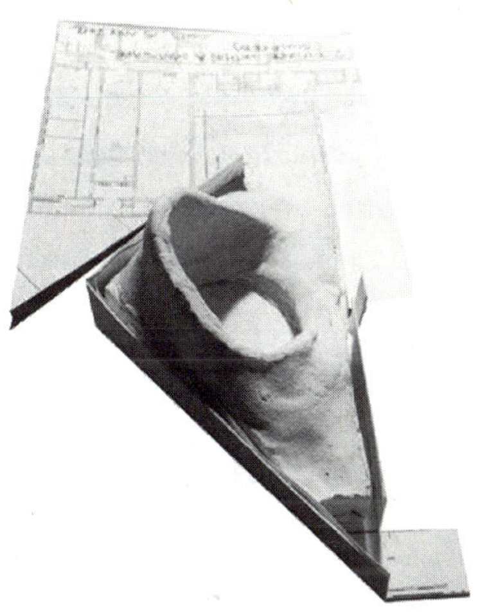

circle. Fold up some card, mold a circular void in a clay mass. Model one.

But you hate circles! Yes, that's true. They imply a vacuum, self-obsession. Even an ellipse is a step in the right direction. It has directionality, at least.

Anti-circle stance confirmed, I crumple the sketch and start over. This time I look at the previous winners and make a bestiary. A woolly mammoth from MOS. A starfish from HWKN [44]. Several bats (a good response to the call for shade). After thirteen iterations, are there any new animals left for this environment?

Back in November, after I had received Barry Bergdoll's surprise call to say that we'd been shortlisted, I spent two days walking around Long Island City and Greenpoint, visiting the scrapyards and manufacturing shops that surround PS1. Jimmy [31] joined me. We collected samples: copper plates with penny-sized circles removed for unknown reasons, discarded motherboards, plastic bins... Between scrap yards, we passed by small manufacturing operations, and stopped to investigate if we saw anything of interest: a New York City taxi repair garage with yellow parts everywhere, an

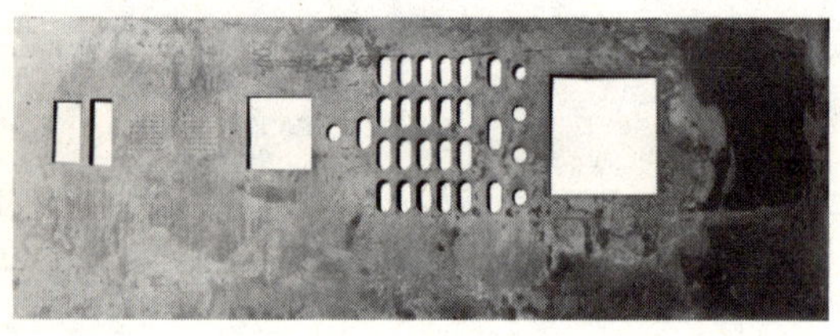

aluminum fabrication shop with shiny leftovers, and an elevator company. Here, we discovered steel panels with punched openings corresponding to the number of floors in the building for which they had been destined, before some minor error was made. They were partially rusted and cast beautiful shadows. But above all, they were waste. I remembered writing in my application: Do not use any materials for this temporary pavilion! Borrow them from an existing recycling loop! And now we had found it. I told the owner's son about the project, and he was enthusiastic about donating their offcuts, but then—

he never returned my calls. Maybe he was worried about how many errors they would need to make in order to meet my material requirements.

Aside from this encounter, most scrapyard owners were hostile and almost physically ejected us. For legal reasons, they said, they could not sell scrap to use. Do you have a recycling license? Can't do it!

We heard it over and over. The only real possibilities were to find legally dubious scrapyard owners (of which there were a few), or to source

material from the manufacturers themselves, like the elevator company. I did not find the right material, but our explorations did give me sense of the roughness of the place. Graffiti, railroads, repair shops, and large steel signs with graphic letters from a previous era. The project should be part of this. That is its true environment: that rough place beyond the walls of the museum.

The next night, I go back down to the basement. The second model is a Trojan Horse. Next, a wall. The horse is my secret favorite. But animal fetish aside, it is conceptually sound: it touches the ground in only a few spots, yet it has the mass to cast a shadow that could create shade without a canopy. A new species for the bestiary?

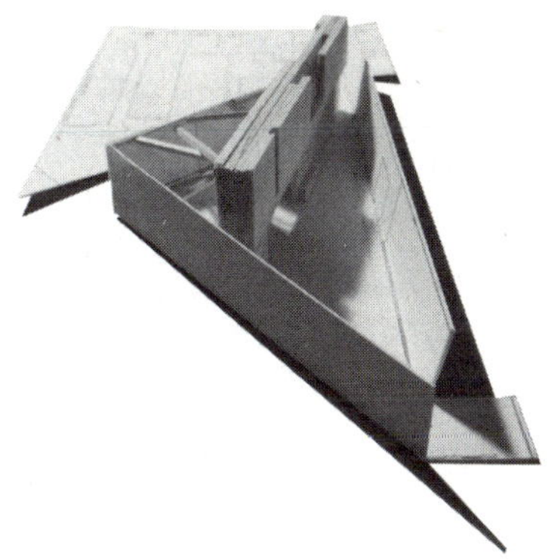

On the other hand, the wall is so bold and simple: a line that organizes the chaotic spaces around it; like the circle did, but without its baggage. The fourth model is a wall-horse.

In all, twelve models are made in the basement before the official start of the project, although one appears by itself and is not made by me. John [29], apparently, has left the ring-shaped design as a gift for me and as a friend for the other eleven. I nickname it "Precious."

When we finally do a workshop with Cornell students and my newly formed CODA core team—Suzanne [119], Michael [69], and Stephen [111]—I present the nomination portfolio, a sun study, the scrapyard photos, and the bestiary. I present Klaus' [42] double brief, stipulate a scale, and send

the team off to design their own proposals. A few hours later, the table is full of models and I slip the basement-twelve into the mix unnoticed. They need to be anonymous to get honest criticism from the students. We whittle the options down to three categories: Precious (John's ring), Troy (the horse) and a series of Wall projects. But better than any of these is Joe's [58] "billboard" wall, out of which the letters WALL have been cut. The sign is all architecture, all-Venturi and all-Eisenman [210], but was equally at home in Long Island City.

The next day we let the little models rest and focus on materials, but over the next few days Troy and the Walls converge. We make larger scale models of two projects to discuss with the engineers: Precious and Wally.

I went to the basement and she was not there

John Zissovici

but I saw all the models neatly lined up on her desk, and some crumpled papers. I don't know if I saw something circular in a drawing or in a model, but it made me think, instead of this poché thing with a void in the center, what if she made something that was a space but also a kind of object? It occurred to me to try that version out. I took a toilet roll tube that seemed to be the right scale and cut it at an angle. I supported it on one of the existing walls (although the later version just sat on the ground). She put the wire mesh on later. Maybe she felt like it needed decoration. Maybe she thought that I was also proposing to build it out of recycled toilet roll tubes and it needed decorating. After she had decided on the WALL scheme she came up from the basement one day, sat down on the couch opposite where I was reading, probably in my bathrobe, and came right to the point. "So, are you going to help me with this thing or not?" I guessed the toilet roll tube scheme didn't count, so I said yes.

We agreed that I could make the video that was required for the final submission. She wanted

the video to show the larger context with the billboards visible from the highways and elevated train, then zoom in on her project. I proposed using Google Earth because I had experience making videos in that medium and was confident in coming up with something compelling and unexpected. She said, “I don’t like Google Earth.” That’s how it was decided that my lasting contribution to the WALL would remain the ghost of the toilet roll tube scheme.

Jimmy Hoffa in the junkyard

James Lowder

In our seven-mile hike that we took around Greenpoint and Long Island City, Arthur was the only junkyard owner who was even remotely interested in talking to us. Of the other half-dozen or so that we visited, most would not even answer the gate. The ones who were willing to talk to us quickly turned dismissive, showing complete disinterest, if not annoyance, at our requests to talk to them about their operations. It became clear that they were already deeply immersed in a system of flows on which their profit margins depended—the fluid yet fast-paced collection of large amounts of refuse material that was then sold and distributed to plants for recycling. They simply were not interested in anything that could potentially disrupt that system.

So when Arthur opened his door to us, which I think was mostly out of curiosity and boredom than genuine interest, it was a welcome surprise. Upon entering however, it seemed unfathomable to me that his was a functioning junkyard, as it lacked anything that resembled a coherent system of organization. It was an intense landscape composed of densely heaped and scattered pieces of plastics, computer parts, dismantled telephones, damaged pipes, crumpled painted aluminum, wires, kitchen sinks, various offcuts of some sort and other unrecognizable detritus of commercial industry. It seemed almost geological in its scale and structure. It was comprised of decades' worth of dumping piles on existing piles, yet there were no discernible strata in these precarious yet looming masses. I asked if he had any idea of what was at the center of these piles, or if the junk got much older towards the back, which was inaccessible, as the valley through the twelve foot tall hills of junk where the path was located ended about a third of the way in to his property. If we dig deep enough, would we find crumpled bumpers of Edsels and Studebakers? Arthur didn't rule it out. "Somewhere in there, if you look hard enough, you'd probably find the remains of Jimmy Hoffa." And while we laughed, the thought of someone being buried in there seemed like a real possibility.

Caroline began by asking some fairly benign questions, to which Arthur provided hilariously obtuse answers. His tone was calm, yet tinged by a contained hysteria.

"Are there moments when you get a lot of one particular material?" she asked.

He paused, looked at me, and then back at her—I think in part out of confusion as to why she was the one doing the talking, and in part for dramatic/comedic effect.

"Yeah," he said, with a smirk and a nod.

"Do you ever get things that could be used as a building material?" He furrowed his brow, and looked at me again. "What kind of building would that be?" he said with an incredulous look.

Caroline laughed. "A small temporary pavilion...for the courtyard at PS1 here in Long Island City. It wouldn't have to be weatherproof or sealed or anything..."

"Uh huh. Well, then... yeah," he said.

"What is your most common material?"

He looked at me again, bemused, then slowly looked to the left and the right at the junk piles surrounding us, and then back at her...

"Depends," he shrugged.

After about ten minutes or so of this, two things were pretty obvious—one, that Arthur wasn't going to be much help, no matter how amusing we found him to be, and two, that this was going to be more difficult than first imagined.

It was clear that there was a push from PS1 for the pavilions to more actively engage issues of sustainability, so Caroline had decided that the way to do that was through materiality, which I thought was an interesting take on the problem. So the question became: is there a way to use recyclable material as a building component? How would that work? Is it a skin logic? A structural logic? How could you use recyclable material without it looking like a pile of junk? How much of a single material would be dependably available in six months? She initially had aluminum bales in mind, but that seemed unsatisfying somehow. Our brief interaction with Arthur immediately showed the problems in working with recycled materials: most of it was small (or at a scale and articulation that didn't lend itself to architectural use), or it had been compromised or lacked a material consistency (and therefore you couldn't depend on its performance). Or, it was all just kind of ugly.

The biggest problem this revealed had to do with the problems surrounding the consistency and stability of building materials, namely that you have little control over what you are going to get and the quantity you are going to get. It seemed like you wanted to get into the process before the material made its way to the junkyard when it is in a purer state, but that promised to open another can of worms...

Between yards, we walked by a taxi repair shop which had racks of bumpers, fenders, and hoods—all kinds of bright yellow car parts that looked promising for a moment. We imagined taking and using them as a sort of structural skin that you could aggregate, all dented and folded in strange ways. It could become a novel architectural skin, but also something that was a readily identifiable part of New York's identity. It would be cool to buy miniature taxi car models sets and play with ideas about kit bashing, but then the same problem arises as before... you have no control over what parts you could get when, it was a closed loop of taxi accidents, auto repairs, and the storage of car body parts.

We didn't find the right material that day. But it was fun to hang out and talk about other things in our lives as we walked through a cross-section of Brooklyn and Queens we had never seen before. How were things with John? Misako and I are talking about moving in together. Have you seen anyone from school recently? Should I start writing essays on architectural representation?

Built that wall

Giffen Ott

From the handful of us sitting around throwing out ideas like "Trojan Horse" and "Gilded Donut," we all agreed that we liked field conditions over the formal design of an object, but when it all came down to a vote, we went for a formalist object, thrust into a field. Democracy does interesting things to values and compromise.

In any case, this was never a democracy—the vote was just a loose guideline for the monarchy.

Parts of the horse and the donut made it through, but eventually the idea with the upside-down letters had the edge. Something about signs, something about misreading, something about a play on words, something about the sun...

Someone—overeducated—misread the upside-down WALL as *Mauer*, as in, German for "wall." Others read something else erroneously in it: MAT, MARR, MITT...

Mauer might have been most accurate from a political-science point of view. Walls divide. But this one—since it was not *actually* a wall, and just *said* that it was. backwards and upside-down—did not.

“Build That Wall” has different connotations today, of course. But at that time, we built that wall.

Wall of ideas

Andrea Simitch

January and snowing. Rand Hall, the architecture department, the entire town all have that hollow feel when the students are gone. Just one hot-spot of activity at the intersection of Milstein Hall and Rand. Lights on and radiators clanking. A handful of students buzzing, pinning models to the wall. A matrix of options for the PS1 installation, all the same scale. Dense on the left, but petering out towards the right, as ideas are exhausted and retired, leaving only a handful to be improved and focused. I give my critique. Other faculty too. We're paid in Martinis. Later that night I sit by the fire and make a collage, inspired by that wall.

The double brief

Klaus Biesenbach

1. The finalists of YAP are asked to submit a design proposal for an environmentally friendly urban landscape for MoMA PS1's large entrance courtyard, made up of three outdoor spaces. The project aims to explore and improve upon the quality of public space by providing elements of shade, water, and seating—and also to focus on themes of sustainability, recycling, and reuse. The courtyard will be used both by visitors on the weekdays and by large numbers of young people during the Warm Up music series of Saturdays throughout the summer of 2013.

2. *EXPO 1: New York* is simultaneously and continuously a large scale international art exhibition. It is an experimental laboratory, a world's fair of information, experiments in the arts, media and sciences. It is an art school, a studio, a kitchen, a garden, a movie theater, a sound space, a summit and a conference, an internet space made tangible, and a space for participation. *EXPO 1: New York* is a new exhibition format that is combining in its display object and performance, learning and teaching, experiments and results, experience and exchange.

The YAP installation for summer 2013 would complement *EXPO 1: New York* by serving an expanded function. It will not only act as a pavilion to host Warm Up, but also function as a flexible experimental space to accommodate 300 people for classes, lectures, conferences, concerts, and performances. Like the VW Performance Dome's role during the fall and spring, the YAP installation will provide a space for a range of activities that go beyond the confines of a white cube gallery, making physical the interdisciplinary nature of *EXPO*.

Notes from a phone call

Matthias Hollwich

Costs more like half million. Do something smart but modest. Wall idea is good.

Liability is an issue. Permit the project? Need to pin down early. If permitted, need general contractor.

Engineer? It's windy there.

Important: Novelty, sustainability, fun-factor, shade...

Don't obstruct courtyard... many people.

Don't make structure inhabitable.

Don't rely on existing wall.

Do something in 2 big courtyards.

Do good video and song.

Do 2 models.

Get Art Domantay [156] as your contractor.

Get team of consultants.

Volunteers: 10 people + students.

Construction time 6 weeks.

Can't do real foundations… use ground screws.

Refined… not too crafty.

Positive attitude!!! Not too academic.

Remember financial and technical.

Klaus Biesenbach.

DJ booth is up the stairs.

Electricity lines in ground.

Fun!

Present last.

Pro-tips

Florian Idenburg

- 30% idea 70% realization
- pick music the jury likes
- present last (tip from Eric Bunge)
- it's about fun, playfulness, and shade
- never propose an inflatable....

Christmas for one

Pauline Morrow

Caroline phoned and said she would be extremely busy and working all over Christmas and it wouldn't be worthwhile coming home for just one day. God! I thought.

I could have gone to Paula's in England, but I was studying myself for a foundation degree in Travel and Tourism Management. I had exams coming up in January.

So I spent Christmas alone. I made Christmas dinner anyway: Chicken, stuffing, carrots, Brussels sprouts and roast potatoes for one. I did a little writing about Christmas with my family long ago, and planned travel ideas for 2013: Cyprus, Rome, and New York, maybe?

I was on Skype most of the day with Paula and Fergal [184] and Caroline, but it's not the same. But I thought, sure, if she wins, it will all be worthwhile.

This could get complicated

Nat Oppenheimer

The design team unpacked two different models from a cardboard box, but it was clear to me that number one was the one. Its letter-like volumes cut

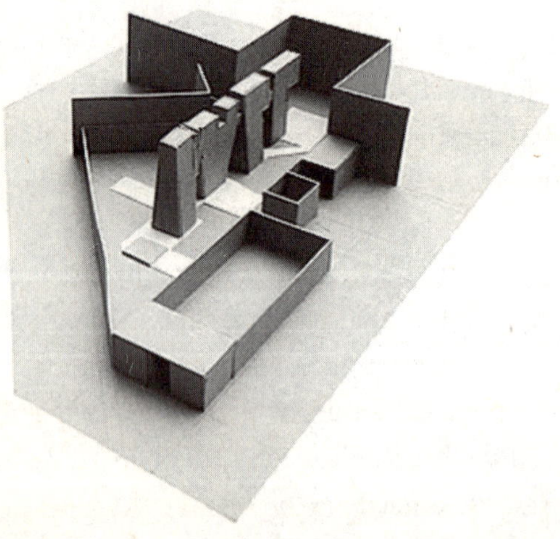

a line through the museum courtyard, and they explained it as having something to do with signs and shadows.

We discussed two structural options: off-the shelf scaffolding and simple wooden truss. They had questions about stability and thought we might need to use the existing building to brace it. This could get complicated, I thought, only because the actual profile of the existing building(s) were not consistent (in strength, material, height, or profile) and suggested solving the problems universally, using water ballast to counteract overturning loads. We had used these sorts of bags a year earlier with ARO's project in Zuccotti Park. In temporary installations, water is a smarter choice than sand, since it is so easy to fill and empty the bags.

I did some rough calculations and saw that wood would get chunky fast because of the bladders' dead weight. So that was out.

In a perfect world we would design a structure with custom steel. But there was no way that was happening, given the budget. It seemed likely that off-the-shelf scaffolding was the way forward, but she insisted on pursuing both steel options.

Although my role was as a structural engineer, I had worked on a few of these competitions before and shared some thoughts—mainly on the issue of budget. They left encouraged that the basic idea was not too far off the grid to work, but concerned about budget. These projects seem to always go over.

A go-between from a cold call

John Sinnott

Three of them showed up at my office. They wanted to know about new ideas in recyclable materials. It had to be fast, it had to be cheap, it had to be local—that was the nature of it. I mean you could start from scratch, but of course that's expensive and this had to happen in a hurry.

So we talked about a lot of the exciting projects that we were developing. I do this all the time with my work—we have state funding for this program, and the Cornell Center for Materials Research itself gets National Science Foundation funding too. We have labs for all kinds of materials research. We have at least one microscope that's one of about five in the world. Nice toys!

After that, we brainstormed ideas that were further afield: what about a company out of Manhattan or Brooklyn that was making this kit-of-parts furniture? Or, a kind of decomposing plant container? Or what about Patrick Govang [52]?—he used to be here with us until he started e2e Materials, the company that owns Comet Skateboards. They developed this technology to use soy-based glue to make laminated wood products. The technology had actually come out of the Fiber Sciences Department at Cornell. Pat then took it and became entrepreneurial with it. He forged a relationship with Comet, and even convinced them to relocate so they'd be close to Ithaca.

By the end of it we must have talked through about fifty different material options. Of everything, they must have seen something special in those skateboards.

A history of bones

Patrick Govang

I had literally just walked out of a meeting exploring what more we could do to utilize our waste when Caroline called us. We had creatively repurposed our sawdust into energy for our production facility and wanted to do more. It was a really natural connection, and things happened quickly. The team came by, and we pulled out some samples of what our "bones" looked like. We showed them how we could readily turn the waste into something useable.

Comet [248] has driven a number of innovations in the skateboarding world since its start in 1997: introducing water-based coatings, using earth-friendlier glues, sourcing our wood locally, buying back and recycling old boards... things like that. The business was never solely market-focused but driven by social and ecological ideals too.

As long as there has been a history of making skateboards, there has been a history of bones. You start with a blank, a long rectangle of wood veneers (thin layers) sandwiched with glue, which is then shaped under heat and pressure into a form. Depending on the design, the form will have waves and shapes and concavities. From that form, we cut out a couple of different shapes for various models, what's leftover are bones, offcuts from the form.

The reality is, there isn't a single effective solution for every skateboard made. There's only a fraction of factories that take those bones and grind them back up into sawdust, which then gets sold to farms for animal bedding, or maybe reprocessed into energy, if they have pelletizing equipment. But it's really hard to justify the long-term expense of

extra equipment, so a lot of companies end up taking the short-term round and paying to landfill the offcuts.

The Wall is by no means the lasting solution to this problem, but my business partner Jason saw the opportunity to raise public awareness around this side of the industry, and highlight ways today's practices could be improved. Skateboarders are historically our inherent rebels driving change—that's where the passion is.

STEP 1: HEAT PRESS

Laminates are formed to one of eight curvatures depending on the skateboard type to be fabricated.

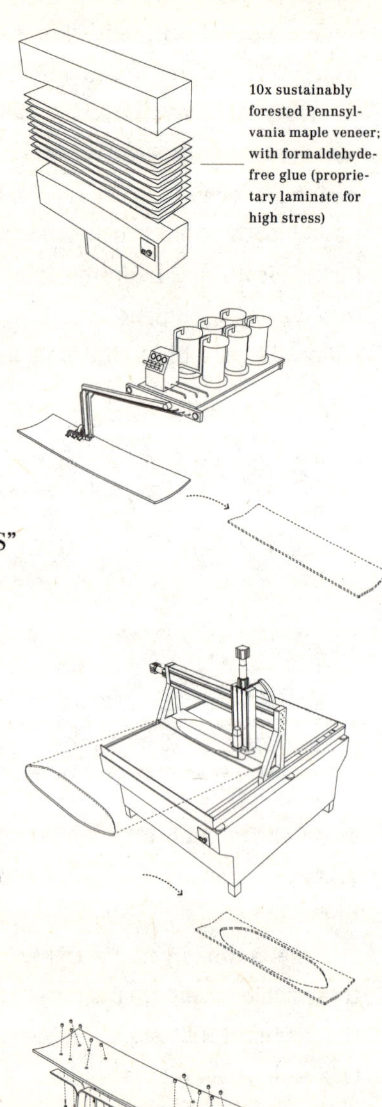

STEP 2: SCREEN PRINT

Boards are printed using toxin free water-based inks.

STEP 3 & 4: BOARDS TO "BONES" AND "BLANKS"

Boards correctly printed are milled according to design, leaving one of eight variations of an O-shaped remainder. The facade is then constructed from these "bones."

Boards incorrectly printed are waste—these "blanks" are utilized as benches that integrate into the facade.

STEP 5: WATERPROOFING

Blanks and bones are treated with highly resistant, environmentally-safe water coating.

STEP 6:
BONES INTEGRATION

Treated bones are arranged in the facade so as to utilize all eight possible shape variations in an interlinked system, minimizing the need for alterations of individual units.

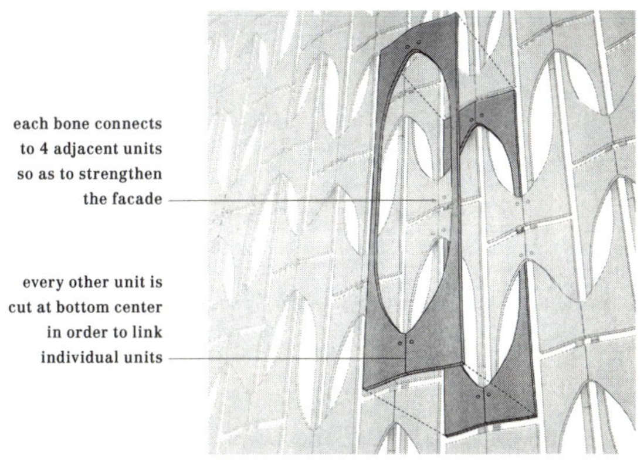

STEP 7:
FACADE STRUCTURE

The facade is hung from steel cables, which run vertically along the periphery of the primary steel structure.

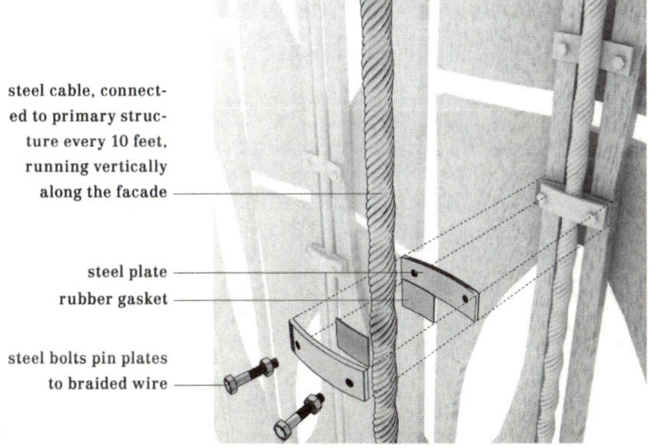

Thomas Trusses

David Rosas

I remember. It wasn't that long ago. Someone recommended that they needed a truss system. Even then, they had chosen someone in the Miami area, instead of New York, which was a little strange. Our equipment is here but you assemble it in New York, which made the trip logistics a little difficult—a little costly.

But we were slow over the summer, so we took a look. For companies like us, projects like this are very small, very fast, very custom, very expensive. It's a recipe that very few people are willing to take on. But there's a community of us who find one another—maybe they're more motivated, maybe they're less risk-averse. You don't just ask anyone. Definitely it takes somebody a little different to do these things.

I was an architect; it's what I did before the recession. When they reached out, my career path was already pivoting toward production. At the time I was new to it—working on temporary structures for projects like concerts, art installations, TV shows, staged events, in- and outdoor, some more custom than others—now, that's all I do for a living.

The equipment we offered is an aluminum truss system: it's lighter, it holds its own, it resists

movement up top, and it doesn't rely on excessive cross-bracing. Even if it's from different places or by different brands, whether it's metric or imperial, it's made from the same stuff. If we'd do it in New York and we needed a couple more pieces, they wouldn't be hard to find. Once it's taken apart it just moves on to the next job, or it comes back to us on the flatbed.

The architects were calm, they were go-getters—exactly what we come to expect. They were realistic about the cost and how it would turn out, which you can get a sense from the first couple renders they sent.

We were one option, but they did their homework. They ended up going with steel, custom over pre-engineered—which turned out to be the better option since it was partially donated. In the end they just built one giant truss.

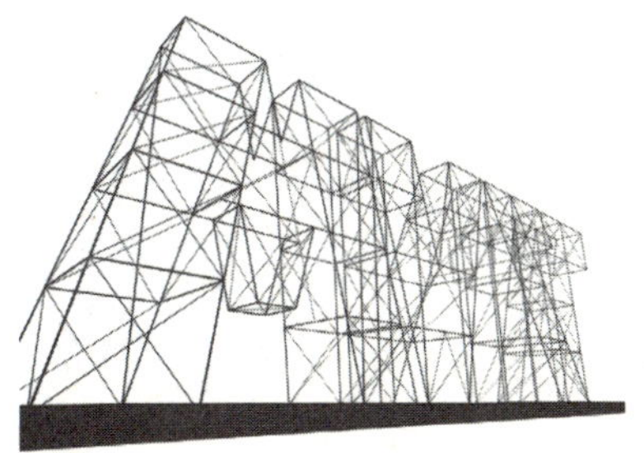

Two weeks

Joe Kennedy

SCENE 1

School shop, after two weeks of weaving tiny, laser-cut, scaled replicas of skateboard bones to create an intricate, lacy facade

JOE KENNEDY: Caroline, do you want to come and look at the skin on the frame

CAROLINE O'DONNELL: Yes

CAROLINE hand on jowls, looks at model in silence

CAROLINE: I am going to the bathroom

CAROLINE leaves

SCENE 2

Caroline returns from bathroom

Caroline: This is not working

We are going to have to go with the flat etched single piece rather than this woven thing

Joe: What's the problem

Caroline: It looks too… country and western…

Joe looks at model in silence

Joe: I wish I'd known this two weeks ago

Caroline: I wish I'd known a lot of things two weeks ago

Delicious, tiny, orange-flavored amphetamine pillows

Rachel Mei-Lan Tan

I had just arrived back after spending a year at Herzog & de Meuron in Switzerland: a year of good manners, proper greetings, and big, grey skies. Back upstate, the sky was also grey. I lived in Simon Ungers' concrete cube house, a grey house, which sat, that winter, on 72 acres of snow-white land.

All this time living in greyscale made the colors of my *Party Wall* work more vivid. Plastic, glitter, Ziploc bags, tin foil, and those fluorescent colors you can never match on your computer to make your background splash pages and line colors, those bright greens, pinks, and oranges. Those early *Par-*

ty Wall days were rich with jarring thirty-minute bursts of amphetamine-level stimulation that kept me awake and on point at all times of the day.

There were important color choices to be made. Going through the virtual shopping cart of Smooth-On to see which colors we wanted for the model pillows, we scrolled down past all the standard colors and found the section for "neon, all the neons."

Later, from a local craft store, I called to ask if we should include glitter to the list. "Yes." Why did I even ask?

After producing the goods and feeling fearful that they looked a little too close to Jolly Ranchers, the response was all-approving: that they had "the proper ratio of wrinkly to smooth" and to "continue making more." They seemed to glow pale orange and everyone wanted to eat them.

These were the all-important water pillows for the required 3/32 scale mock-up. They needed to be as life-like as possible in representing what were to be LED-projection-lit, reflective, half-ton containers of water that would be suspended twenty feet in the air to hold down the entire structure, while there was a party going on underneath it all.

Those delicious, tiny, orange-flavored amphetamine pillows were never realized. They were the only major change between the competition design and the built work. They turned out to be self-supporting teardrop shapes. Blue in color. Those would have been delicious too.

Short shorts

Nathan Friedman

Thurs Jan 3 — PS1 moves up the final submission date from January 20th to the 14th. Six days struck from our Google doc timeline. After a ride on campus-to-campus I arrive to Rand at 6pm. The team is all business. There is a structural debate (tubes, angles, I-beams?) and C (that's what I call her) sets the L-section dimensions at 6" x 6" x 0.5" for legs and 3" x 3" x 0.375" for bracing. We revise the Rhino file and send it out to our pro bono renderer. He's grown frustrated by a steady stream of revisions and threatens to abandon us. I head back to Mike and Sue's apartment in Dewitt Mall. We drink a leftover bottle of champagne from their New Year's engagement and I sleep on the couch.

Fri Jan 4 - Thurs Jan 10 — I use C's credit card like it's my own. We all do. She says if we win, Thai take-out will be the least of our budget issues. Model dimensions are confirmed for the 1/64 urban model, 3/16 project model, bench prototype and full-scale facade mock-up. Apparently half the game is showing up with the most stuff, and that's what we plan to do. I move my bag from downtown to the Simon Ungers cube. Days are spent in OMA and nights spent with the echoes of OMU. We scroll through American Apparel models wearing short shorts and *Party Wall* T-shirts; I realize that our scheme has a life outside of Rand Hall. My request for a Speedo option goes unanswered by our American Apparel connection.

Fri Jan 11 — All final material is to be submitted to C by midnight. The model facade is tricky and we go through five options. In the end we laser-cut and spray paint it gold. I still have to finish the exploded axon and model base. Three years after graduating I find myself back in Rand Hall asleep on a sheet of blue foam. C is napping next to me, and not for the first time.

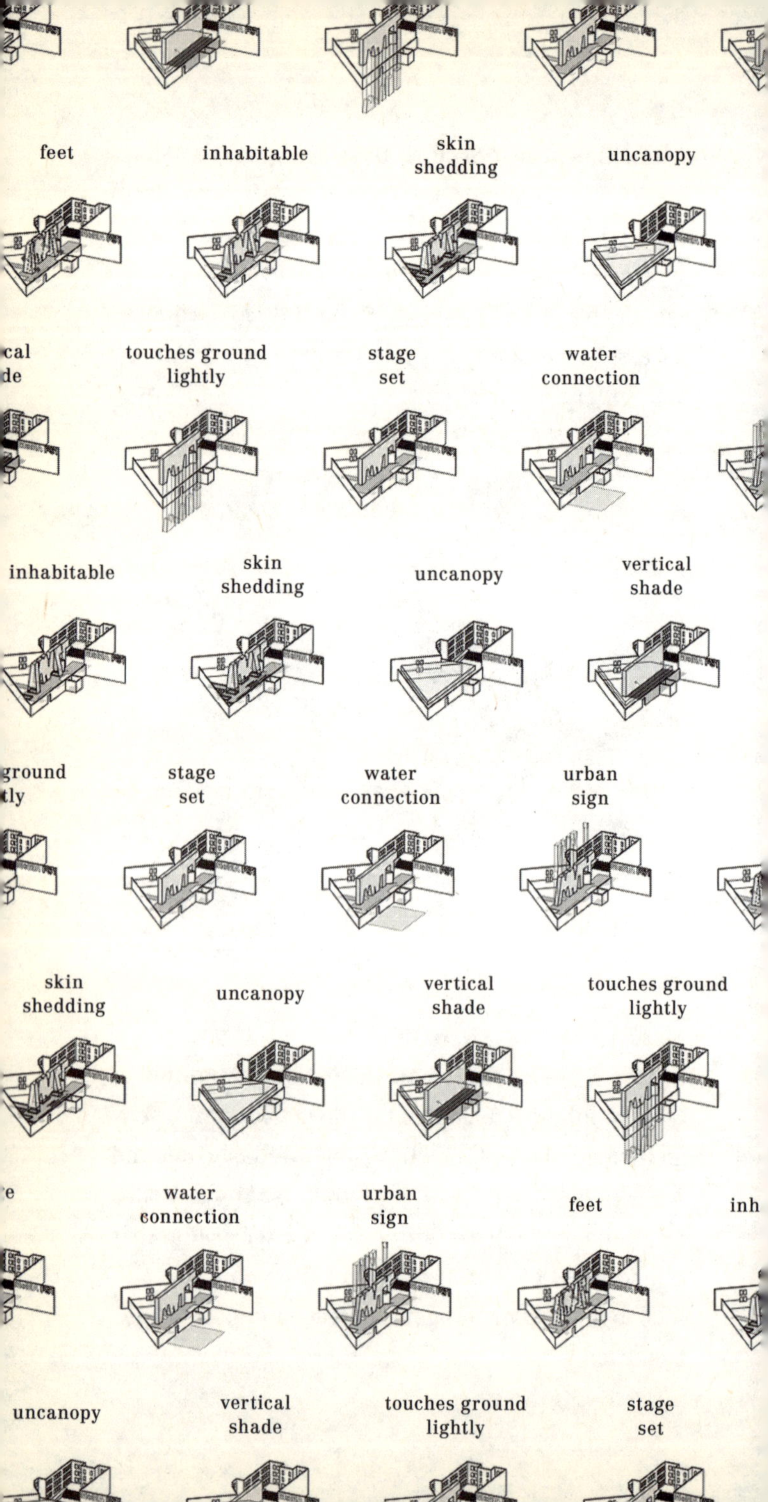
feet
inhabitable
skin shedding
uncanopy
touches ground lightly
stage set
water connection
inhabitable
skin shedding
uncanopy
vertical shade
stage set
water connection
urban sign
skin shedding
uncanopy
vertical shade
touches ground lightly
water connection
urban sign
feet
uncanopy
vertical shade
touches ground lightly
stage set

The word I was looking for

Steven Chodoriwsky

I arrived in Ithaca two weeks before the term began. Snow was coming and going, though no students seemed to be around just yet. The first time I came to the department, Charissa was showing me around the School. After a midday walkabout, we passed through the Milstein studios, at the hinge where the fancy new part fused itself to the old, proud Rand Hall. It was there that Charissa introduced me to Caroline, who happened to be working on a competition. I recall her wearing excessively comfortable boots, winter-ready, like pajamas for feet. So there was not *nobody* around: there was one professor, and a group of students, offering up their holiday time. It was my first experience, in quite a while, of witnessing that prototypical architecture school thing: students huddled around a small group of desks, around models and facing computers, serious and weary. Deadline eyes. And around them a ton of light, fluorescent light, sunlight, snowlight.

So it was for the PS1 competition; I had heard of it. To witness a competition in the thick of itself from just outside it is very exciting indeed. Inside, perhaps exciting is not the exact word. We talked a bit, then Charissa peeled off back to the office, and Caroline brought me downstairs into the shop, where there was a full-scale mock-up of the woven wood offcuts from the skateboards. I remember being shown drawings that were nearby, diagrams of what the thing did architecturally, wondering what it did in reality. The work must have been near the end of a rather long haul, compressed into a tiny slice of actual time. Something something wall. She spoke of the architectural concept. I nodded; I was mostly trying to figure out where I was in the building. Ground floor? Basement? Which building is this again? As Caroline spoke, I remember at one point saying something like, "...and yeah, it really makes a lot of sense, dealing with this idea of byproduct—" at which point her eyes sprang open. "Byproduct!—that's the word I was looking for..." as if I had told her the place she had lost her keys. That word was around here somewhere. Surely it was there from the beginning, but got temporarily lost behind a pile of paper or a wood offcut. She was preparing the final text reports while directing the drawings while coordinating who knows what else simultaneously. We exited the shop, and she headed back upstairs to the team, but not before giving me advice about where to get lunch.

Née Wally

Jessica Levine

Precious, or Wally, or Trojan Horse? That's the question about the name of it. We sit together at the border between Milstein and Rand Halls, testing names. We eat Thai food together at a dining table of drafting tables and make overly personal confessions. I call Ben Weitsman & Son, Inc. about screws, while Rachel [60] makes bladder pillows at

one-eighth scale that look like hard candy. We drink *Gimme! Coffee.*

Then it's New Year's, and Michael and Sue get engaged. I work on diagrams while Caroline makes sketches. I watch the promo video they are making every time someone else does. We get pizza and pop, we populate our pictures with American Apparel models. I overuse the word "peeps"—a technical term for people cropped for use in a rendering.

I work on the book. I work on the book cover. I get files from everyone, sometimes on a USB key in the shape of a skateboard. There are updates to the updates to the updates. And files have names like FINALFINALTHISTIMEIMEANIT. Caroline leaves us positive negative notes, like:

Jess
I don't like the patterns ...
yes ... not any of them.

Yet, the book gets done. I get donuts. I get a parking ticket.

Then I am the driver of the team because I have the biggest car, a mini-van. Wally just fits. I drive 228 miles, or 397 kilometers, south, fog the whole way on the highway. It's nighttime when we arrive in the City and another team is unloading their materials too. We try not to peek at the other submissions but we peek. Then we get something to eat at Mission Dolores and wonder what to do next with our lives.

Where did you get that song?

Michael Jefferson

I was relieved to hear that we were in talks with Chiaroscuro (not their real name) to do the animation for *Party Wall*. We had watched the film that they had made for a previous YAP winner. We had watched several previous winners' films, but that was the one we kept coming back to. It was slick and sexy; the music was mellow and cool; it panned and cruised around a fully rendered pavilion. It was really professional and I thought to myself: I don't want any part of making something like that. I studied film in my undergrad but am no aficionado. Still, architects always think that I can make films for them.

We knew our concept was strong. The project was about urban context: how you see the pavilion within the city, from the highway, and from the train as it passes by Five Pointz's graffitied facades. So while Sue and I were in New York for some meetings—an official one with Richard [145] at PS1, and a sneakier one with the next-door neighbor whose property rights the project might be invading—we took some test footage from the 7-train and from the highway. Riding and driving all day, the microphone recorded our back-and-forth bickering about what

shots to take, from which angles, and even about the legality of the whole operation. Our plan was to give Chiaroscuro the footage to splice into their slick animations. We called them on our drive back to Ithaca, but they seemed ambivalent; for a while they talked more to each other than to us, deep in a discussion about standards and ownership.

It was no surprise when, two weeks before the end, they backed out. Caroline met with Stephen, Sue, and me in *Gimme! Coffee* downtown. It was Saturday and we were taking a break by working in a different place. After coffee was distributed, we were given the news: Chiaroscuro was out. Caroline told me I could do it and looked like she believed herself. I felt faint—but didn't think of saying no.

The next two weeks I worked fourteen-hour days. The project team was structured so that every member had their own responsibilities and ownership: film, facade mock-up, drawings, casting of resin pillows, securing of sponsorships. Every few hours I would get up and walk around to see everyone's progress. It was like opening little gifts. Did the pool boys in the renderings have new outfits? Was the bench prototype made? Everyone trusted each other to do their part. Thosc fun moments kept me motivated to make the film, despite my exhaustion—and despite the fact that I was about to propose to Sue.

Meanwhile my little film team grew. I called old colleagues for advice. Noah joined the team, and while I dealt with the overall editing, he rendered the long panning shot fifty times. It didn't seem like the most efficient way of doing it but we didn't know how else to do it. Jerry [80], a Cornell grad and now the Architecture Visualization Workshop Coordinator, was put to work on the rendered and special effects portions of the film. Jerry wasn't a fan of the project. *This is never going to win*, he'd say—but not in front of Caroline. Lastly, I talked to Beardo [75] (our nickname for the amazingly talented Juanito, who had an impressive beard at that time), a professional renderer I'd worked with at OMA. He wanted nothing to do with the film, but we did persuade him to give us three great renderings—for a very reduced fee and some unmentionables.

The film begins with an arrhythmic percussion, and flashes through various urban scenes: shots from the train and highway of the billboards and graffiti, interspliced with renderings of the project from the same moving vantage point. It then cuts to a long tracking shot, meant to de-emphasize the pavilion itself and focus on the activities it generates. The Wall is rendered as a line-drawing, and figures are rendered in various colors. The chairs flickering on and off—actually fifty pieces of film edited together—appear to pop off the facade, all in time with the popping beat of Zammuto's song, "Yay."

For the last scene, the melody swells as the camera rises up from the dance floor to an aerial perspective. Finally, looking directly down, the wall itself becomes a line cutting through the courtyard, and what we see now is its shadow, which reads, "WALL." The final reveal, the music drops, the credits roll.

PS1

What we didn't know how to do, we figured out. Finally, a few days before the deadline, the team gathered and sat and watched the film. And again. Then someone else arrived, we watched it one more time. It really energized people. Even Jerry started to think we could win. He made a few extra renderings to add to Beardo's collection: *We just might win*! Any time anyone came by, we watched the film again. After all this work I expected some recognition. The most common reaction was: *Where did you get that song?*

The song was a digital staccato that Caroline didn't like at first, but I fought for it. (She wanted something more '94 ecstasy-inspired techno, which she finally gave herself in the "making-of" video.)

In the end, I felt liberated by Chiaroscuro. By stripping it down and communicating the idea not through glossy animations but with our own limited means, it made the film raw and powerful. It told the whole story in two minutes and thirty-six seconds.

I sat in on the jury presentation with the engineer. As one of the multiple flexible uses, Caroline showed a slide of a wedding, and told the jury that, by the way, two project leaders became engaged during the process, and would be happy to fulfill this programmatic requirement. They were actually in love, she said, it was not something they were doing for architecture. We were, and we did.

At the end of the film, the jury was smiling. They got it! Klaus Biesenbach asked the first question:

Where did you get that song?

Freedom

Juanito Olivarria (Beardo)

they gave me almost complete freedom with the images, with cameras / time of day / entourage etc, and i feel that's why in part the images turned out well. i was surprised when i received the photos of the structure from the opening party because of how much the project stayed true to the renders. (no guy selling balloons however.) after working on the winning project, next year's winners (The Living) contacted luxigon to do their images and we won again. not saying its a sure thing but, if you want to win, my email is—juanito.olivarria@luxigon.com

The way water works

James Garland

There's a moment when you exit the plane and the fragrant air hits you. Your body settles. You're surrounded by water. That's what it was like, landing in Hawaii.

From there, a couple days later, I drew some rough sketches for a water scheme while the design team was working in grey Ithaca. I was on Christmas vacation with my family.

The opposite of laminar flow is turbulence.

I had looked through her website; it was clearly conceptual. But there is concept and there are the details: there, that's where our business is. If things don't work there, the whole thing is a wash. And the way water works, there's no room for error.

It's often that you demand a lot from the details, but they demand a lot of you, too—it's like they're putting your concept out there on a gangplank. Well, that's a bit severe. Maybe it's more like we share a teeter-totter.

Consultant work is an art form.

But if you stay too long under the mist, the individual droplets make a bridge, becoming a continuous surface. They hang together, hooked on the skin. All of a sudden, you're soaked.

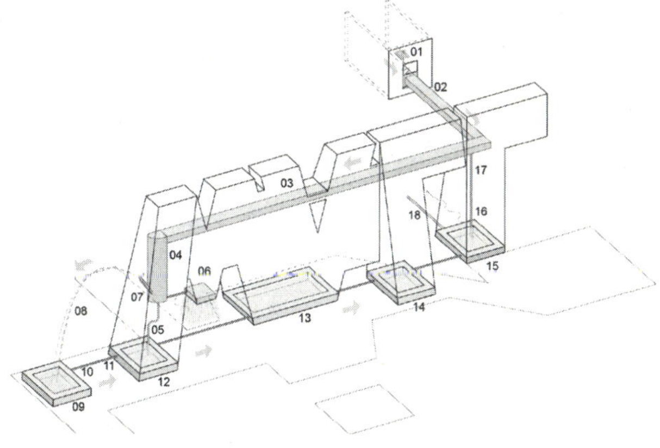

01 WATER SOURCE
bathroom connection; start-up & make-up water

02 AQUEDUCT 1
channel into waterfall drop to aqueduct #2, +/-40' long

03 AQUEDUCT 2
channel to pressure tank, +/-90' long

04 PRESSURE TANK
+/-15' TALL, 12" diameter

05 OVERFLOW RELIEF LINE
to pool below

06 MISTING STATION*

07 ANGLED STILLING CHAMBER
quazi laminar nozzle

08 CLEAN ARCHING STREAM
breaks into rainfall to pool, 3/4" diameter

09 CHURCH POOL

10 CHURCH POOL OVERFLOW
to low profile runnel

11 LOW PROFILE RUNNEL
connecting all pools

12 WALL POOL 1

13 WALL POOL 2

14 WALL POOL 3

15 WALL POOL 4

16 SUBMERSIBLE PUMP*
to recharge aqueduct 2

17 PIPE
up to aqueduct 2, +/- 25' tall

18 PIPE
to drain

Never

Jerry Lai

This project is never going to win. Never. Ever.

They just won that

Scott Hughes

They just won that, I thought, as the jury filed out of the presentation room. I haven't been to many of these, but I was pretty sure. Looking at Caroline, she seemed pretty sure too. The jury asked questions that were about realization: was this really possible? Could *we* really do this? And they seemed jovial.

Nat [48] had a scheduling conflict and asked me to step in for him at the presentation. I made it just on time, rushing from one of the six or seven townhouses I was working on in Brooklyn. I had never met the designer before, but I knew that she was the person I was looking for as soon as I saw her: anxious, dressed in black. I had no sense of the part I was to play, so it was a relief when she said that all I needed to do was field questions.

Would enough skateboards be manufactured?

Was there a problem of air rights over the neighbor's property?

Why would Banker Steel [135] *want to donate all of this material and labor?*

Caroline answered most of these. Then:

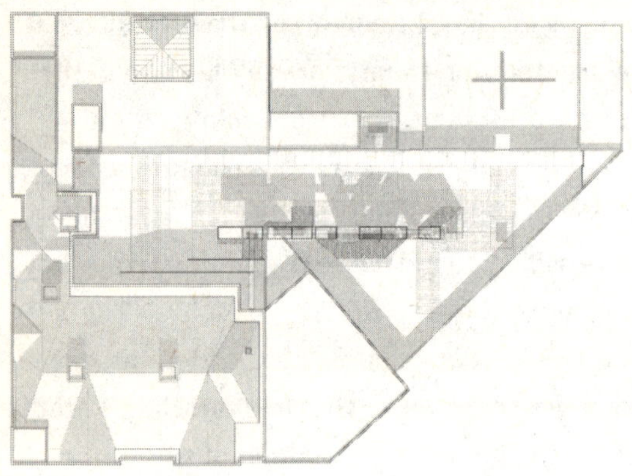

Roof plan

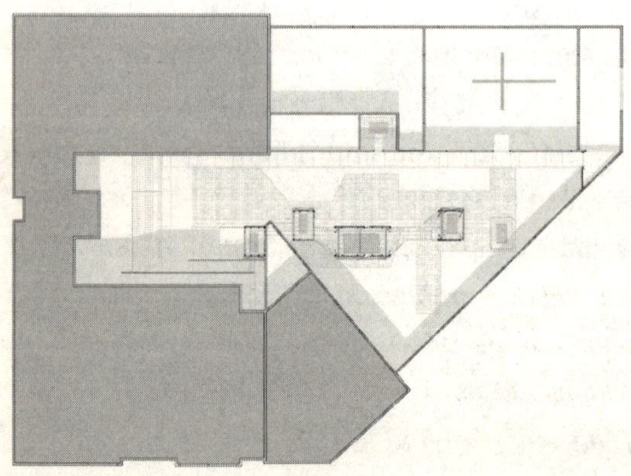

Ground plan

What if there was a hurricane?

Would this giant wall tip over?

And what were these water pillows actually doing to help?

At that point the footings were nothing more than leveling pads: twelve-inch-deep concrete that would do little for overturning loads. I explained that the water bags were to counteract the possibility of overturning, and that we had used them before with ARO at Zuccotti Park. I told them that Silman Associates had worked with Banker Steel before and had complete faith in their promise. I told them that the structure was designed to withstand 60-70 mile-per-hour winds. I assuaged their fears.

At the time, I didn't know that we would end up using seven-foot ground screws, greatly improving the resistance to the overturning load, or that the ballast would be teardrop-shaped bladders instead of the pillows the renderings showed. I didn't know that we would use leftover steel, or that we would engineer the structure to match the steel, rather than the other way around. I didn't know that in

MOMA

the end Banker would not be able to provide all of the manufacturing at no cost. I didn't know that the transition from Rhino to Revit models would not go smoothly, or that we would lose our steel detailer before even starting. I didn't know that we would make on-site changes due to badly-fitting bladders, or hastily add diagonal members to a wracking "L" as a storm approached. I didn't know that I would stand on the PS1 balcony at the opening party, champagne in hand, getting the same view of the structure as I had of the model on the table of the presentation room as I fielded questions.

But I was pretty sure that we had won.

Squatting

Mikey Loverich

The damn thing won't extrude properly. Plastic keeps coiling up around the nozzle, making the extruder look more like a pig ass than a good investment. My elbows hurt from propping my head off the hardwood floor where I lie, belly down. Melodic music comes from the printer and is supposed to inspire thoughts of new beginnings, but it just makes me sad as every chirp and chime means another failed print, another oozing nozzle I need to wipe. This is one machine that loves to rub failure in my face. After returning from travelling through China and India, I've set up shop on the floor of Jimmy's very comprehensive architectural library, waiting a couple weeks for a subletter to move out of my own apartment. My camp consists of an inflatable mattress and pump, a duffle bag, four walls of books, and a 3D printer. The printer is my new toy, bought while in domestic limbo and guaranteed to bring me joy. But all it has produced so far is frustration.

As I lie there a woman peaks into my room, illuminated only by the printer's glowing LEDs. At a glance, my room has all the qualities of a rave: blue electric light, dark space, strange odor, mysterious sounds. But with further exploration, one can only see—heartbreak. To this woman I must look like a troll, conjuring precious plastic gems from a machine that smells like honey. Or someone madly in love with a glowing box. Whatever she *thinks*, it doesn't matter, because what she *sees* is the floor and bed covered with failed extrusions and used clothes, all gleaming in blue light and reeking of *huā jiāo* that I brought back from China.

She widens the cracked door and introduces a far more foreboding foe into my camp—light. It blinds me. All I see is her silhouette as she leans against the jamb.

"Knock knock, what is going on here?" she asks.

"I'm embracing the future," I force out, embarrassed to be startled in my present aesthetic state, and not willing quite yet to engage with a human. I had heard a nomad would be in the apartment the next few days, in NYC working on something big. Something secretive and cool. I, a bit jealous even though I know nothing and hear only whispers, appreciate the comfort my dark lair provides.

"Well, cool, I'll be sleeping on the couch, we should hang out, out of this... *room*... sometime."

"Yes, later," I mumble, turning back to a new beep, another deformed creation.

We do hang out later, but always hovering around door jambs. And with her competition win, I take much more credit than I deserve. I tell myself I'm not so much a troll but a caught leprechaun—one with precisely two more wishes left to give.

Things from things

Pippo Ciorra

We've been going on together for three, four years, and we're really happy, and we've had very good results. Of course YAP goes everywhere now, and we've begun in new countries—like Turkey or Chile, or now, Korea. Juries have a great vantage point on what's happening over a wide geographic field, and it's easy to get excited. But the funny thing is—wherever we go, we always agree. There's never any tough discussion. Strange, considering all the cultural conditions, their backgrounds, their ambitions. We must be near a time of change, then, because it's become too easy to choose, every year, from the first moment.

Generally—and I've sat on juries in New York, Rome, Istanbul, Santiago, Seoul, so I have a certain record of experience—we are finding a condition of interesting architecture. I wouldn't say it's quite comparable to the early years of YAP in New York, when there was this kind of booming formalism—but now—everybody's more accurate. Entrants take it seriously, they want to build, they know the construction process, they're smart about budgets. And there's not much money. So it has to be serious...

And PS1 is a party place, no? There isn't that museum aura you'd find, say, across town at the MoMA. But now, the projects in different YAP locations around the world are becoming more comfortable with being in a museum. Young architects are more prosaic; they require less conditioning; they are conscious of this dialogue with art, and their architecture stands there, as with art, at one-to-one. They even approach works of art, in terms of really understanding their social commitment or their aesthetic role. But at the same time, the projects get more practical, and we think this is good.

And young architects can get the best out of this situation without getting involved in the discussions about the divisions between art and architecture—like at the end of the nineties, for example. That's all a little bit useless now. Young architects can be architects.

Think of the difference: all these established architects at the end of their careers, they don't really want to build museums anymore, they want to be in museums! Whereas these young architects—they can start from the museum—instead of being this final, auratic task of their careers—and then bring their success out into the world.

The chances that young architects have to do something with a high level of integrity is very low. You are often not sure whether you can have it outside. And once you prove you can have it, it's important that you once again go outside and see what happens. You can use that experience to convince people that you can access results and integrity at the same time.

The museum is also a terrible test. You put this thing there, people look at it and use it, they see whether they like it or not. It's demanding, but also gives you an immediate response. So if we consider the frame of the museum as a rite of passage condition, I think we can accept it much better, no? This

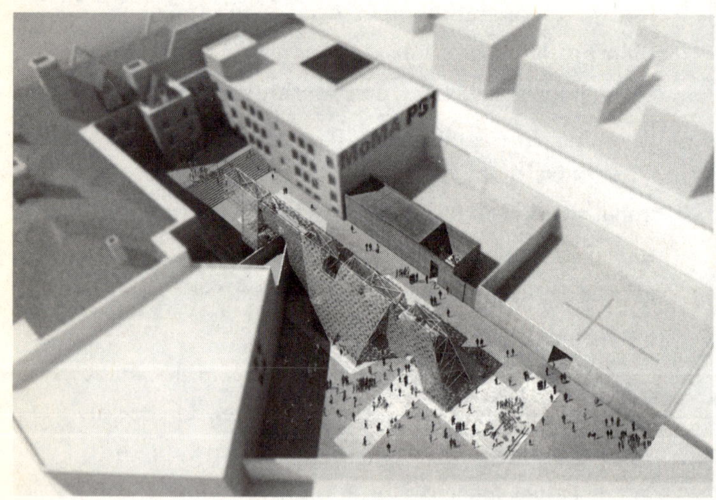

is what the museum can offer the young architect.

Meanwhile, what the young architect offers to the museum is architecture's flexibility. You can respond to different conditions. It helps us to kill the boring discussion about the thing and the representation of the thing, because this architecture is both at the same time.

In the architectural world today there is, I think, a striving to find theories. This is getting very fashionable. We are all looking, coldly, for ideological forms—but without ideology. But my answer to this is: you can work with the idea of making things from things. You can work on this if you accept that this work can be done by recycling elements, and reusing and reshaping can be as monumental, as

important, as strong, as new… as the new. Architecture is like a protean form: time after time, it takes what it has, uses what it finds, and transforms itself into other architectures.

This was what I liked about CODA's project. It's where my sympathetic nature for the project comes from. The idea of making a significant presence in the landscape using small-scale recycled elements—that was incredibly interesting for me. They're using vernacular elements, everyday objects, using and recycling waste, but at the same time doing something very monumental. In a way, it makes up for its "Trojan Horse" aspect.

And when you use a skateboard, you're basking in the landscape of the city that is brought inside the courtyard to you. The scale of the thing is what made them win, but it's not even the scale—it's the dimension of the thing, it's its urban impact.

There's another quality—it could be conscious or unconscious—but it states an approach to an architecture that could never be a style. I mean, the next time CODA will do something, it will be completely different. We're beyond what Peter Eisenman in the 80s would call "the problem of authoriality." You don't require recognizability, you don't have to spot the architect, young or otherwise, anymore.

II

The Design Development

Not just a pun *

Kelly Chan

This year's winning design for the MoMA PS1 Young Architects Program (YAP) promises to deliver another grand 7-train spectacle this summer, with a temporary pavilion that gives last year's ginormous, anthropomorphic, air-cleaning starburst *Wendy* a run for its money. *Party Wall*, conceptualized by Ithaca-based firm CODA, addresses the annual YAP prompt of turning PS1's sun-baked courtyard into a pleasant summer hang-out by building a permeable barricade/shading structure using recycled wood from an Ithaca skateboard manufacturer. Like last year's winning design, *Party Wall* impresses first with its sheer size, gamboling over the permanent walls of PS1's schoolyard and announcing itself to a larger urban radius beyond the confines of PS1 (the video flashes footage from the 7-train, which provides elevated views of the PS1 courtyard that *Wendy* certainly reveled in).

What we didn't know until we saw the video was that the immense pavilion offers a tongue-in-

* "CODA's 'Party Wall' at MoMA PS1 Is More Than Just a Pun (It's Two Puns)" was originally published in the Object Lessons blog at ArtInfo.com, March 15, 2013.

cheek architectural joke that is bigger than the pun in its name. We knew that the curious shape of *Party Wall* was certainly not arbitrary, and it likely served more function than to provide oddly cut-out chill zones for PS1 visitors to park themselves. We'll let you watch the video to find out what other party tricks this "wall" can do (Hint: the answer starts around 1:40).

How far out from your shell you stretch

Peter Turner

As a college business officer for a multi-million dollar enterprise, you stick your neck out every day for various projects, and sometimes for people. How easy you make it for your head to be lopped off—how far out from your shell you stretch, and why—is always interesting to reflect on. For *Party Wall*, we felt way, way out there at various times, and not until the safe and on-time takedown was confirmed to me on September 9, 2013 by the Chief Operating Officer of MoMA did the Dean [13] and I finally take a deep breath.

It started routinely in late 2012. Professor O'Donnell had entered a MoMA-sponsored competition. She needed to use model-making and computing facilities ordinarily closed over the winter break. She asked for a renderer from the College IT staff. Done. She needed authorized shop staff and prior approval for model sizes, materials and run durations. Sure. The professor had student volunteers standing by, she had asked nicely, she anticipated the administrators' issues, and answered them in her first communications. She thanked us often. This is what we are here to support, isn't it? Frankly, we don't see enough big idea proposals. Go for it!

You what?
You won?
One hundred thousand dollar budget?
Installed in five months?
It's how big?
A book-thick contract?
$3 million of insurance required?

To this point, O'Donnell had positioned her competition entry and potential MoMA relationship as being from her sole proprietorship—CODA. Not the best idea, we thought. Complicated as it would be, we convinced her to alter course and set the project up under Cornell's sponsored programs umbrella. MoMA agreed to sign with Cornell. Professor O'Donnell's rights and honorarium were protected. The resources of the University and the Dean became more available. In Ithaca, Cornell's College of Architecture, Art, and Planning would provide warehousing, assembly and office space, tools and hardware, pallet transport to the City, and accounting services for all the Ithaca-based activity of the project. The Cornell Department of Architecture provided stipends for the several teaching associates who were seconded to the design team. In New York City, with the involvement of AAP alumni affairs and the AAP Dean, O'Donnell arranged for structural design by engineers who are Cornell alumni, steel fabrication to be donated by another alum, and actual steel erection on the MoMA PS1 site. A separate construction firm was to lead the facade sub-project to mount the 180 panels onto steel. Steel painting, concrete footings, bladders, lighting, landscaping, and disassembly and disposal sub-projects all needed pro bono donors, or reduced fee deals in the City. Deals or not, every one of these suppliers had to be contracted as a supplier to Cornell and that is never easy, especially without a competitive design and bid process.

So the business team in Cornell/AAP faced down a mountain of what we affectionately call ‘big red’ tape, including relentless correspondence where off-loading worst-case liability was every participant’s goal. We had been guessing we could buy extra insurance if needed, through Cornell, for less than $10K. At one point, just weeks before construction at PS1 was to start, we were facing a $60K estimate from Cornell insurance suppliers. The contract was still not signed as lawyers on all sides weighed in, all imagining worker accidents and hurricanes:

“Peter, we have not yet received the purchase order for this job. We are starting the work on Tuesday and need to get the insurance certificates in place prior to starting.”

“Peter, bladder costs have escalated by $20K. The detailers backed out, and the fabricator has decided to charge, versus donate.”

“Peter, please sign this agreement as soon as possible ... needs it immediately in order to start the preparations on their end."

"Peter, yes, you can proceed ... with the understanding that we do not have an indication on the cost at this time but the cost of the insurance will reside with AAP."

In the end, our Risk Management and Sponsored Programs leadership came through for us. We met the requirements of the contract and signed with MoMA, and then internally decided how to comply using excess plus additional insurance. The underlying insurance from the subcontractors, which we eventually uncovered in our contract negotiations with each, helped in the final insurance shopping.

Some days you think you do this because you're dumb. On good days you say to yourself you're gutsy, even fearless. But the truth is: you persist behind the scenes because of the possibility to be part of something fantastic. *Party Wall* was fantastic. You know what else—honestly? The heartfelt thanks given publicly at the June 27, 2013 grand opening in New York City—and privately on numerous occasions to all of us behind the scenes—made it all worthwhile. Most faculty never thank administrators.

I'm ready for the next big idea.

Seemingly impossible dreams

Mike Moyer

Throughout my seventeen years as a fundraiser, I have been privileged to be a part of gifts that have reshaped great universities and their respective colleges. I have worked for these universities matching alumni and friends' passions with the priorities of the university. When priorities are ambitious and reach across boundaries, then fundraising goes from a fun job to a thrilling and terrifying ride.

Party Wall, it seemed, would take a heavier lift than CODA's preliminary budgeting had anticipated. $100,000 more, in fact. So they called me.

When many professors—and deans for that matter—walk in to my office with a project that "just" needs $100,000, I try to dissuade them from thinking it will be successful. The road from zero dollars to $100,000, through gifts from multiple donors, is much harder than one thinks.

The good news is great ambition drives philanthropy. *Party Wall*'s ambition tapped into the pride of our alumni base at an elemental level. They were proud that Cornell had a professor who had achieved the winning design in this prestigious competition that is so much a part of New York City. She was one of theirs, and they were going to see her succeed. The New York City donors also had great pride in realizing this project in their own city. They did not need recognition— save the knowledge that one of the most important annual design events in New York City, and the world for that matter, was brought to fruition by a Cornellian.

For the next six months, we worked tirelessly to talk with alumni and friends of our College to raise the funds to bring *Party Wall* to reality. The project brought familiar alumni together from across the university. But the provocative design also drew new friends for the university. We told the story of reusing local skateboard waste, of vintage signage in Queens, of reprogramming space through facade to bench transformations, of hidden messages written in the shadows. Truth be told, it was easy: once people heard her story, then they wanted to be a part of it.

I am in Virginia now, but a piece of *Party Wall* still hangs on my office wall. I take great joy in telling the story every time someone asks, “Why do you have a skateboard on your wall?” It reminds me to keep my ears open for the moment that the next person walks into my office with a project that has seemingly impossible dreams.

Early advice

Alexis Lenza

You have a really tight window for construction. That is the very first thing I notice. I work on constructability, reviews, working on small mock-ups, contextualizing forms—things like that.

You come to my office one day with a small mock-up model. Call it a peer review. So, I say, hey, have you thought about a better way that this, or this, could be put together? A different pair of eyes for a change of focus.

Early advice is everything.

In this industry, until you get the contractor involved, you don't really know where things are going to end up. It takes time for you to find the right person, the best means, the best methods. I'll speed that up. Here are some names. They tend to have cost-saving ideas, time-saving solutions. You'll need one contractor for the foundations, and one for the panels.

That's the thing: you aren't afraid to build a real structure, good sized, forty feet high.

We look together at figuring out how to do a temporary foundation that would support it. You'll need a bit of something to hold it in place—even though wind will pass through it in places, there's still the possibility for a sail effect, to lift this thing right off the ground.

You're working with Silman, a structural engineering firm here in the city, they have a good reputation. They're working on some options for a screw pile, down into the ground, getting more friction. Great.

Let's review some of the connections of the panels to the structure. Down to even one panel you've figured out, quite literally, the nuts and the bolts.

That hinge between abstract and reality is, very simply, the working-out of a design through trial and error, putting together something you can touch.

I've learned that over time. In my past career I'd been involved in projects where the abstract design decisions had just gone too far. But now, I try to impart that level of constructability early on. It starts with the designers, if you're able to rewind a bit. Some really take that on, take that into account. It pays off in the long-term.

Okay, here are my recommendations. I'm putting you in touch with some installers here who specialize exterior wall systems.

All we wanted architecture to be

Nicholas Cassab-Gheta

All the students at school were talking about "Skateboard Saturdays." *Vice* was coming to do a documentary about us. We were promised Ray Bans that never came. Even so, architecture was cool again. The combination of long boards, sunglasses, documentaries, PS1, DJs, and architecture just seemed so right.

At first glance, the weave of skateboard bones we were producing for the facades was almost incomprehensible—but after one or two thirty-bone panels, anyone could show up and become a pro.

The assembly process became easier every week. After each session, we'd get together for an exit meeting and identify improvements. Each Saturday, there'd be a different set of screws, or the order of assembly would shift slightly to make the process more efficient. Exit meetings optimized our assembly, but above all else, it gave us all a sense of agency. Now, the hard work of all those mornings felt like something to write home about.

I can look up at the wall and know that some of those panels, woven and screwed together in a cold Ithaca warehouse, have my pizza-grease fingerprints on them.

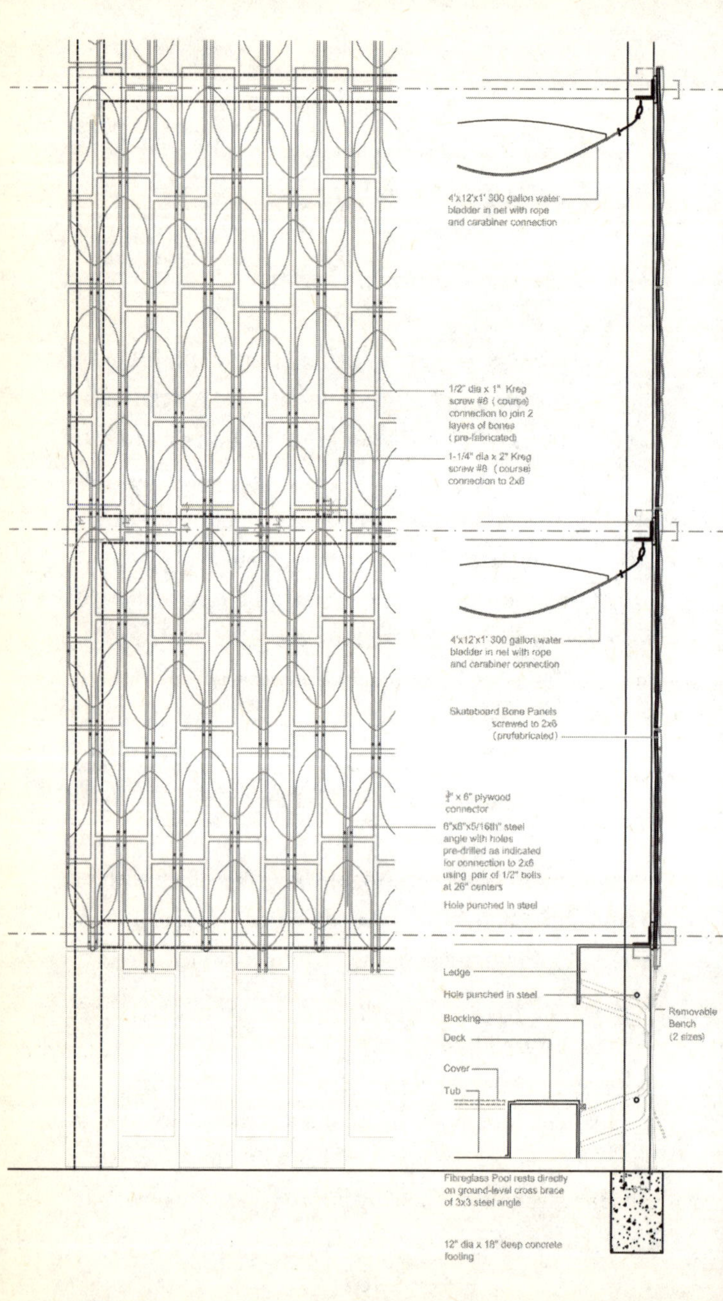
4'x12'x1' 300 gallon water bladder in net with rope and carabiner connection
1/2" dia x 1" Kreg screw #8 (course) connection to join 2 layers of bones (pre-fabricated)
1-1/4" dia x 2" Kreg screw #8 (course) connection to 2x6
4'x12'x1' 300 gallon water bladder in net with rope and carabiner connection
Skateboard Bone Panels screwed to 2x6 (prefabricated)
3/4" x 6" plywood connector
6"x6"x5/16th" steel angle with holes pre-drilled as indicated for connection to 2x6 using pair of 1/2" bolts at 26" centers
Hole punched in steel
Ledge
Hole punched in steel
Blocking
Deck
Cover
Tub
Removable Bench (2 sizes)
Fibreglass Pool rests directly on ground-level cross brace of 3x3 steel angle
12" dia x 18" deep concrete footing

A minor oversight

Stephen Clipp

After taking the lead on facade design in the competition (which was actually chairs at first), my main task in the lead-up to installation was to prepare the woven skateboard facades. Since the design was almost entirely dependent on the donated materials, our state of affairs was tenuous all along: from the tight timeline, to the organizing of weeks of volunteer work, to all the watching and the waiting for things to simply come together.

This undertaking was an incredible, often humbling window into the opportunities and challenges of repurposing materials in architectural construction. From the minute we were awarded the commission a weekly ritual of construction began, in which the materials were collected, sorted, assembled and stored by an entirely volunteer team. Our entire work schedule lived and died by securing access to materials whose acquisition we could not directly control. The fact is, Comet is a small operation, and it makes all its skateboards to order, and those sales are seasonal. Our work could not be seasonal. We had to be assembling our facade constantly just to finish on time. As the boards were produced, we would take the offcuts and assemble them. But there was a minor oversight on our part—no one wants skateboards in January.

Quickly we exhausted our initial reserve of board offcuts. We began to see our intricately orchestrated schedule slip back day by day as we waited for Comet's production to come alive again in the spring. There was a point where it really seemed that we would not have the approximately 3000 boards that our design had called for. In our scramble to keep the engine of facade production churning, we sought any opportunity to get the materials we needed. At one point, to try and make up the shortfall, we received a stack of skateboards from a company in Philadelphia whose form was similar, but incorporated plastics into their pressed laminate. This discolored their bones, and gave them an entirely different flex pattern. The fact that we spent

hours attempting—and failing—to find a way to incorporate these apocryphal materials into our subtle woven facade highlighted our desperation in that moment. Caroline even thought she would have to buy a thousand boards from Comet—just so they would go ahead and produce them, and then resell it to them.

That would have been absurd in so many ways—but we were desperate. But lucky for her Comet caught on, and they helped us out. In those last days of construction, all buffer time had long been exhausted, and our fabrication was a day-to-day sprint. A handful of bones would come in, and we would immediately assemble them, and hope that tomorrow we would have some more. We were weaving them together right up until the day before we had to bring them to New York. In fact, I remained in Ithaca right up until a week before the *Party Wall* was to be completed, assembling the final panels even as the site construction was well underway at MoMA.

Any creative undertaking that attempts something new and novel ventures off the beaten path of fabrication, and will encounter the unforeseen hurdles long smoothed away from conventional production. The constraints of the commission and our own ambition pushed us to down the road less traveled. According to so many people the whole thing went so well. But what most people won't ever know is at how many points the project flirted with failure. We learned many lessons in this project, but the most resonant truth I walked away with is that though the road less traveled leads you to flirt with failure, it's the only reliable route to somewhere exceptional.

Cheeseman

Ben Kessler

After weaving skateboard bones all day at the warehouse, I got a ride back to school. Caroline was going to Wegmans. Did I want anything? Yes, some cheese. Brillat Savarin. She was impressed. I didn't really want it, but it felt like she wanted me to give her an errand. She brought back Brillat Savarin, very proud of herself. Payment in cheese.

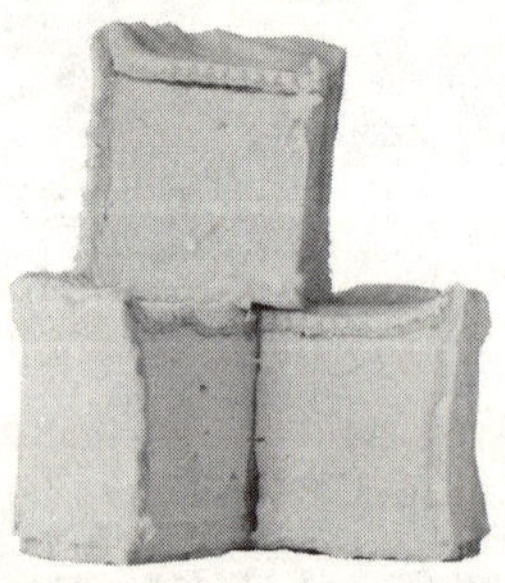

But it was the wrong cheese. It was Brillat Savarin Frais, the fresh version. It was good, but not what I had wanted. I had not specified. My fault. I told her. She did not know my name, only that I was a volunteer. She calls me Cheeseman for the next three years of school. My name is Ben.

Not that kind of girl

Yeung Shin

It became a ritual every Saturday to wake up and wait for Jessie's phone call. She was picking me up for a drive down to the warehouse to weave bones. I made sure to drink liquids sparingly so as to avoid the temporary plastic outhouse.

Once I arrived, I hesitated. While everyone else dove right in, I was always one step behind, intentionally. You see, I am not a drilling kind of girl. Any electrical machine with a metal part in motion is good enough for me to look the other way.

Everyone else seemed to be adjusting their motor skills quickly to the repetitive task: screwing together interwoven wooden scraps, piece by piece, of what would become a wall spanning more than a hundred feet. Not wanting too obviously to appear to be the weakest link, I joined in. Eventually. No injuries, for me, or, in the end, for anyone who dared to walk beneath.

me, Bryan (4)	**Hello** - Bryan@ExtraPackaging.com > > From: Suzanne Lettieri [mailto:se.lettieri@gmail.com] > Sent: Saturday, May Inbox	5/6/2013
Caroline .. Caroline, me (8)	**FW: bladder** - Bryan@ExtraPackaging.com > > From: Suzanne Lettieri [mailto:se.lettieri@gmail.com] > Sent: Tuesday, April Inbox	4/30/2013
Caroline, me, Bryan (3)	**FW: missing piece** - Bryan@ExtraPackaging.com From: Suzanne Lettieri [mailto:se.lettieri@gmail.com] Sent: Monday, April 29, 2013 6:20 Inbox	4/30/2013
Bryan, Caroline, me (22)	**Pics of completed prototype** - Toll Free 1-800-872-7548* (O) 561-999-1860; (Fax) 561-999-1864 Bryan@ExtraPackaging.com ** ** ** ** Inbox	4/29/2013
me, Bryan (18)	**Call?** - Bryan@ExtraPackaging.com From: Suzanne Lettieri [mailto:se.lettieri@gmail.com] Sent: Thursday, April 25, 2013 10	4/25/2013
me	**Additional hose questions** - -Can we connect them together? =is there a valve that allows us to shut it off? thanks Inbox	4/18/2013
me	**shipping?** - Hey are they shipping the prototype today, I need to know when it's going to arrive and when we Inbox	4/18/2013
me, Bryan (2)	**Update** - OK with change? > > Thanks > S > -- Bryan Kramer Extra Packaging Corp. Bryan@extrapackaging.com 561-999-1860 Inbox	4/16/2013
me, Bryan (3)	**Hardware** - > > > > -- > Bryan Kramer > Extra Packaging Corp. > Bryan@extrapackaging.com > 561-999-1860 >	4/15/2013
me	**FINAL DECISION** - Hi, So we've decided to go with a mixture: 3 big (9.5 ton) and 4 small (4.5 ton). This way we car Inbox	4/15/2013
Bryan .. Ricci, me (8)	**Final revised Invoice 37050 from Extra Packaging, Corp.** - bryan@extrapackaging.com] > *Sent:* Monday, April 15, 2013 1:32 PM > *To:* Ricci L. Curren; 'Suzanne Lettieri Inbox	4/15/2013
Bryan .. Ricci (20)	**Invoice 37322 from Extra Packaging, Corp.** - Bryan@ExtraPackaging.com From: Ricci L. Curren [mailto:rc62@cornell.edu] Sent: Monday, April 15, 2013 9:47 AM To: Bryan	4/15/2013
me	**(no subject)** - Just got an email that Cornell will call you shortly with cc info. Here are our options at the moment Inbox	4/15/2013
me, Bryan (2)	**9 ton prototype** - Bryan@ExtraPackaging.com Original Message From: Suzanne Lettieri [mailto:se.lettieri@gmail.com] Sent Inbox	4/15/2013
Bryan, me (4)	**RE: Price Cert labex-ml.doc** - Bryan@ExtraPackaging.com > > From: Suzanne Lettieri [mailto:se.lettieri@gmail.com] > Sent: Monday, April Inbox	4/15/2013
Bryan Kramer	**Hose info** - See attached for the hose 'specs'- I am told they are aluminum connections. You will get 4 Inbox	4/12/2013
me, Bryan (7)	**Prototype arrival** - Bryan@ExtraPackaging.com > > From: Suzanne Lettieri [mailto:se.lettieri@gmail.com] > Sent: Thursday, April Inbox	4/11/2013
Caroline .. Paul, me (12)	**RE: Party Wall detail** - Bryan@ExtraPackaging.com >> >> From: Suzanne Lettieri [mailto:se.lettieri@gmail.com] >> Sent Inbox	4/11/2013
me, Melinda, Ricci (3)	**Water Ballast Payment** - Hi Melinda, Bryan from Extra-Packaging will be sending a new invoice today for the remaining six Inbox	4/11/2013
Bryan, me (4)	**RE: Order post prototype** - Bryan@ExtraPackaging.com >>> >>> ** ** >>> >>> Original Message-	4/9/2013
me	**Order post prototyoe** - Hi, what do you think the turnaround time will be post prototype? We're concerned about getting	4/9/2013

I had an affair with two men

Suzanne Lettieri

I had an affair with two men during my short engagement to Michael. I will call them Bladder Man One [125] and Bladder Man Two [127], because that is how they were affectionately known to me.

Between the three of us we exchanged more than 500 emails between January and June. When I look back over those correspondences now, I feel… well, sweaty. The all-caps words we used in some of the subject lines pull out many charged moments:

FINAL DECISION (April 15, 2013);

BLADDER FLIGHT SCHEDULE (May 10, 2013); and a particular highlight—

DRIPPING FROM ALL SEAMS (June 10, 2013)!

As the chronology of his nickname suggests, I got in touch with Bladder Man One first, back in December, while we were working on the competition. Silman, our engineers, had suggested using "water pillows"—I searched online and found a company called Interstate Products. Sean (not his real name) told me that he grew up in Queens and when he was a teenager he had had a water bed.

He loved it so much he started this company. The standard bags he could provide were affordable. Rachel went to work modelling little yellow pillows, and Silman set about calculating.

I had originally been assigned to work on designing the structure, but I was spending so much time phoning and emailing Bladder Man One that Caroline took over the steel job and I became bladder-exclusive. A lot of my time was being consumed not by the bladders themselves but in finding cargo nets that could support them. Nets such as these existed, but due to the weight they would carry they were more expensive than the bladders themselves. It would have been almost half our budget for nets alone, and that didn't make sense.

Silman connected us with Bladder Man Two, who was willing to look into a self-supporting bladder. Bryan (his real name) lived in Florida and liked the beach. These teardrop-shaped bags were more aesthetically pleasing, but in order to get them for a reasonable price, they would have to be made in China—Bladder Man Two had never made these before. In the end, and despite the risk, cost was a good excuse to use the better-looking products. We ordered seven yellow teardrop bladders.

The choice had huge implications on the design of the steel. Originally, seven nine-ton bladders were designed to hang in the seven vertical shafts of the Wall. Whereas the pillows and nets would need holes in the steel at every horizontal intersection, the teardrops would need to be hung from a central point. Delays in the bladder decisions delayed the steel.

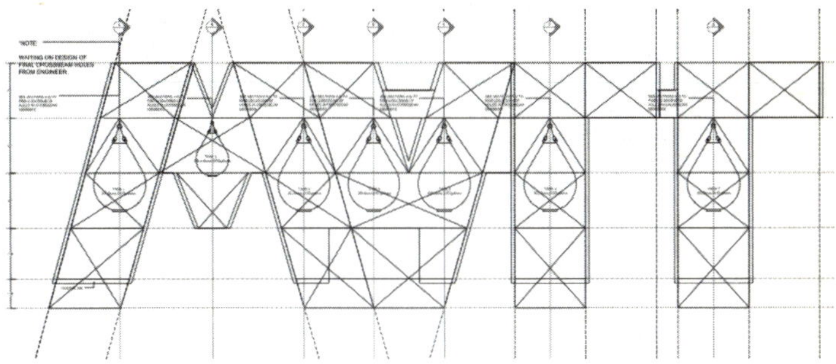

Along the way, communication was tough. I would ask a question one day, Bladder Man Two would talk to China in the middle of the night, and we would respond the next day. It could take three days to answer a simple question.

The first signs that there would be problems came when Bladder Man Two forwarded photos of the first test bladder. In the photos, what looked like a male-model was standing with his shirt half-open next to the sewing machine in the Chinese factory, and outside, an old woman with groceries was walking underneath the nine-ton teardrop. It looked great! But it wasn't yellow—it was black.

By the time we relayed this, they had already continued with the other bladders. Because of time, we realized we had no choice but to let go of control of the color, and told them to just continue with the black ones. It was not what we ordered, but we needed them on time and we needed them all the same color—which color exactly was secondary.

The test bladder was already on its way to us so it could be tested on-site. When it arrived SFDS hung the huge black bladder in the small courtyard and filled it. Eric [159]—director of SFDS and former circus rigger—never believed that we needed the bladders and didn't trust them. As if proving him right, the canvas straps started to rip through the plastic-coated fabric almost immediately. Despite his mistrust of the product, Eric thought that the ripping was only due to the asymmetrical way the bag had sagged onto the ground, and thought the others would be just fine.

Meanwhile, as the steel and foundation designs progressed, Silman allowed us to reduce the loads in the bags. We proposed a new layout of large (nine-ton) and small (four-ton) bags. When a shipment of bladders arrived, Caroline and I eagerly opened the packages in the loading dock. They seemed to be packaged in blue plastic, until we unraveled them… They were all blue. I called Bladder

Man Two. Just keep going with blue, I told him.

With bladders in hand, and more en route (blue, I was assured!), I wondered what I would do on site, now that my work was done. The steel structure was complete in the first two "L"s, and Ryan [163] was busy installing the facade hardware and hanging the first bladder. We had a water permit to use the fire hydrant to fill the first bladder. It filled quickly. It leaked immediately. I called Bladder Man Two.

Ryan, who was originally the "lighting guy," was by now overseeing everything under SFDS's jurisdiction. Whereas the panels and steel were running smoothly, he spent most of his days on site trying various fixes on the bladders: rehanging, filling, emptying. Day after day they leaked. I called Bladder Man Two.

Bryan had many ideas, and insisted on sending me a box of polymer that would partially solidify the liquid. It was a product used in hospitals for solidifying liquid waste. Ryan was reluctant to use it because it meant that, in the end, the resin would be more difficult to get rid of than the water. He persevered, though, and made new, custom gaskets for the bladders and resin-glued the interiors. One by one, he fixed the leaks.

But what if the water evaporated? I called Bladder Man Two. He proposed we make little hats for the bladders. I sent him a sketch.

"Like this?"

"Yes."

He spoke to China. Hats ordered.

As the steelwork progressed we could hang more bladders inside the structure. By now, we had received a replacement for the black teardrop, so that all but one of the bladders were the smaller four-ton size now. Still, the straps were much longer than specified and they hung down below the level we expected. This was not a problem in the two "L"s, but the cross-bracing in the "A" would clearly intersect with the bladders. The engineer came to the site and called his colleague back in the office to run some numbers. Within ten minutes, he told us we could eliminate another bladder, meaning four small bladders in total.

After the demount, the artists in the *Colony*, (a77's live-in installation which was occupying the small courtyard) took the bladders. One of them was sent to an organic farm in Jersey. I got a call from Bladder Man One: could he buy one of Bladder Man Two's bladders? Finally Bladder Man One and Two were talking to each other and I stepped out of the relationship. I had to get married in less than a month.

Bladders

Bladder Man One

Back and forth with Sue. Back and forth, we tested various kinds of bladders. People think they're made of rubber, but really it's this awning-style material, rubberized.

We built some prototypes, filled them up, this size, that size, showing the shape they'd hold, how their different weights would affect different surfaces, and sent back a bunch of pictures and

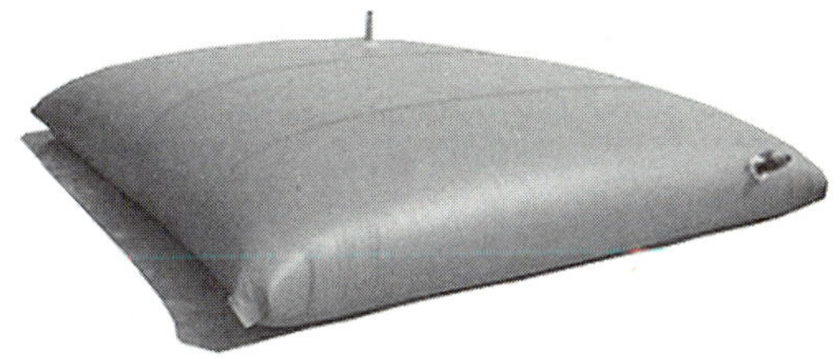

numbers. The basic shape we tested was a pillow shape. Originally they'd be held in a netting, which turned into platforms when the netting became too difficult. But that's as far as it went.

They ended up with bladders in a teardrop shape—but that wasn't something we were doing. Liquid bags is one thing, that's our business after all, but not the whole system to carry that load.

I'm no engineer, and I don't play one on TV.

Sure, I wish I could have been more involved in the end-product, but it wasn't something I was prepared to try out live. Especially not to hang it above people's heads inside an upside-down wall. That made me a bit uneasy.

Afterward though, I actually bought one—I just wanted to take a look at it! I hate to say it, but the quality of what they bought shows the location where it was made. I'd never seen anything like it. They used some molded-plastic-style fittings where I definitely would have used a finished hoop. They had a loop on the bottom and the straps tied in a knot. I wouldn't have put my name on something like that. It did hold its shape, I'll give it that.

Bladders

Bladder Man Two (Bryan Kramer)

Now that it's over with, I can be honest. It started off fun, and it got stressful real fast, especially at the end.

Extra Packaging is my father's business. He's been doing custom projects for forty years. I was in the concert promotion business, but after ten years of his guilt trips, I gave in, and moved back to Florida. I said, you know what? I'll give it a shot. And this was my first big project. No one else was available or capable of dealing with it, and it was loosely related to something we sell in inventory—that's how Suzanne found us. We sell a product called Aquatank, which is a small bag made for drinking water:

Water becomes an even more precious commodity after a natural disaster such as a hurricane or earthquake or after a man-made problem. Water supplies can become contaminated, and the loss of electricity can prevent the running of an electric pump. Reliable storage of emergency water supplies is thus an essential component of hurricane preparedness. The Aquatank was designed with this problem in mind. [...] *The*

Aquatank is the ideal water storage alternative to 55-gallon or smaller drums. The Aquatank water container is compact and easily stored, using no more space than a pizza box before being filled with water. Aquatank water containers and water bags are manufactured with FDA-approved, food-grade material as an economical solution for storing and transporting water.

Somehow this description fit CODA's bigger idea of what they were doing with the project. But over time, rather than just buying a bunch of our pre-made tanks, it morphed into this complete custom project. It took us months and months of emails and phone calls just to get to this... shape. Originally, Suzanne supplied me with a drawing that showed a standard, square, pillow-shaped bag, but then, after a ton of back and forth, she asked, you know, couldn't this ideally be a self-supporting teardrop type of thing instead?

Well, that changed things! A teardrop is totally different from a pillow! The pillow would have rested on nets with cables and hooks and all sorts of accessories—it would not have been pretty. And it turned out to be expensive, too. Suddenly, the teardrop solved both problems. We could just hang them from a single point.

We decided on a design that already existed, making it a little different and a lot simpler. But it was not a simple order at all. There was a lot of heat sealing. Not one thing was sewn. To customize involves a simplification that is really complex.

The bladders were made of PVC-coated fabric, like an inflatable boat. Their straps were polypropylene, like seatbelts only thicker, like a woven cargo strap that you've probably seen on big trucks. They're rated for certain amounts of weight as well as for torque. For hanging water, there's a certain

amount of pressure, but if there were to be an earthquake, it would be double the pressure, so they're made to withstand those kinds of shocks.

Their sizes kept changing and morphing. At one point she was asking for bags that held nine times something we were already making. Then I

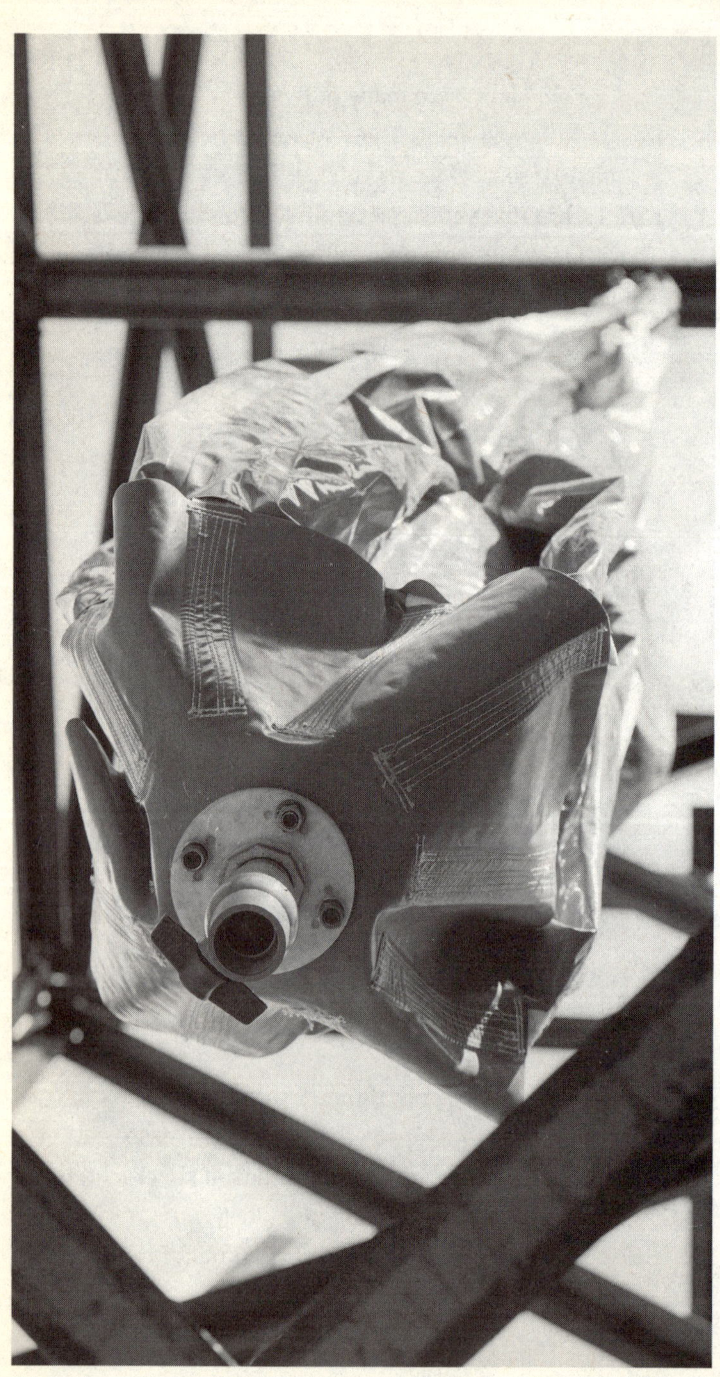

tried to persuade her to buy a bunch of pre-made three-hundred gallons ones, but it would've been overflowing with tanks, floor to ceiling.

Ultimately, the engineers reconsidered some of the math due to changes in the foundations, so we ended up with these four-ton bladders, still way bigger than our Aquatanks. Going down from nine to four was a relief. After all, these things were going to be hanging there for ninety straight days, above people's heads. Nobody's done that before.

The prototype didn't leak, but once it was approved, the rest of the bladders leaked—more or less. It was obnoxious. Suzanne called every day. She kept sending me photos of leaking bladders. I don't know what happened, or what changed, but something changed; they dripped and dripped and dripped.

But one day, the photos stopped. They got them to stop leaking. They just glued the exit valve closed. Genius.

Best partner

Emeco

On Thurs, Dec 27, 2012 at 4:57 PM, Emeco wrote:

Dear Caroline: the project looks terrific. But I am not sure that Emeco is the best partner for the seating element. For us to tool up and make 150 sets of legs for a one-time use is not in line with our production set-up, nor our philosophy.

I noticed in your presentation you identify "contradictions" in the MoMA brief. Here's another: 300 chairs, cheap enough to get for free, use, then throw away, yet environmentally sound, and with some design integrity. That is a very tough assignment.

However, I really like the way the "scales" of the upside down WALL shed to become the seating. I just don't know of a process and material inexpensive enough to do that.

*

On Wed, Feb 6, 2013 at 4:23 PM, Emeco wrote:

Hi. We can make the legs for 120 seats (480) for $1600 total (NIC hardware). See the photos of a mock up attached. The leg is very strong and durable—tempered and anodized aluminum with a Lexan foot cap. The design is like the leg on the Alvar Aalto stool—simple and you can use it on many sizes. We took your wood thickness at 1/2-inch—be careful about the screw getting enough meat, but not coming out the top.

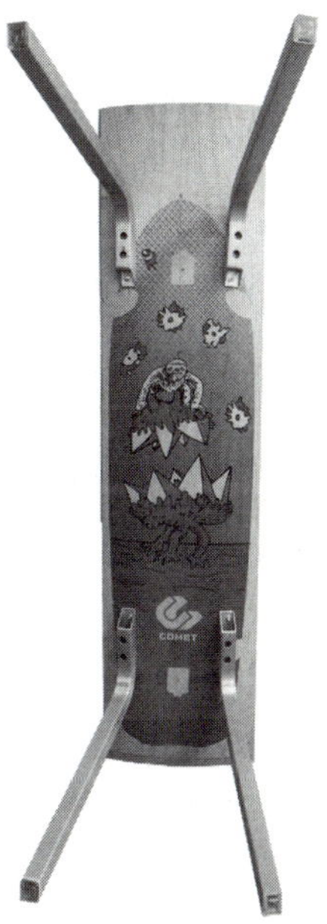

We only have room for two screw holes (not three like the Aalto stool)—so I recommend screws and glue. We will need a little time to tool for this so please let us know as soon as you can.

We are happy to help in this small way.

*

On Wed, Feb 20, 2013 at 3:36 PM, Emeco wrote:

We can align the screws per your drawing.

We cannot alter the plastic glide (these are already a standard part). We cannot make each leg with a different angle.

We can make the legs 3/4-inch taller.

By copy I am asking Denis Tangen if he has any thoughts on getting the legs to touch the ground evenly. What happens with weight on the bench? Do the legs "flatten out" or get more off kilter?

Let's see how this goes, and maybe we would be interested in working with the skateboard company. The legs would be more expensive for any other use besides the MoMA project.

Smell it

Chet McPhatter

This may sound odd, but the steel fabricator is like the rock star of the construction business. Before we show up to build the framing of a structure, no one can truly picture what's going to be there.

And another thing: ironworkers are also the most entertaining people you'll meet. They have great life stories—but getting into their inner circle can be tough.

Normally, Banker Steel wouldn't get involved in a project this small, but one of our employees, a Cornell alum, asked us to help out. With *Party Wall*, it looked cool, we like complicated work, and we pride ourselves on taking care of our employees and customers. We fabricated each individual element in that complex little structure using leftover steel in our yard: hundreds of connections, hundreds of punched holes.

That reminds me: my family has this corny saying—"when the wind blows, smell it." And that's what we did here.

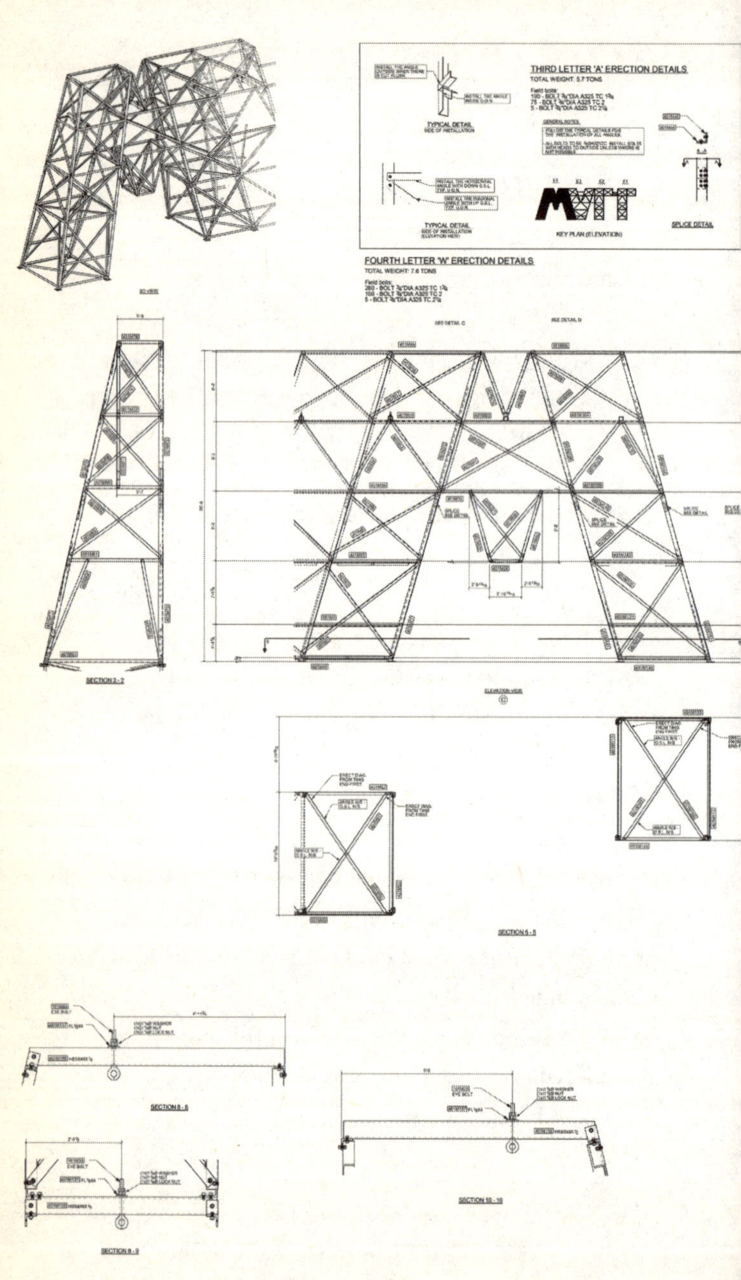
3D VIEW
TYPICAL DETAIL
SIDE OF INSTALLATION
THIRD LETTER 'A' ERECTION DETAILS
TOTAL WEIGHT: 5.7 TONS
Field bolts:
100 - BOLT ¾"DIA A325 TC 1¾
75 - BOLT ¾"DIA A325 TC 2
5 - BOLT ¾"DIA A325 TC 2¼
GENERAL NOTES
TYPICAL DETAIL
SIDE OF INSTALLATION
ELEVATION VIEW
KEY PLAN (ELEVATION)
SPLICE DETAIL
FOURTH LETTER 'W' ERECTION DETAILS
TOTAL WEIGHT: 7.6 TONS
Field bolts:
280 - BOLT ¾"DIA A325 TC 1¾
100 - BOLT ¾"DIA A325 TC 2
5 - BOLT ¾"DIA A325 TC 2¼
SECTION 2 - 2
ELEVATION VIEW
SECTION 5 - 5
SECTION 8 - 8
SECTION 9 - 9
SECTION 10 - 10

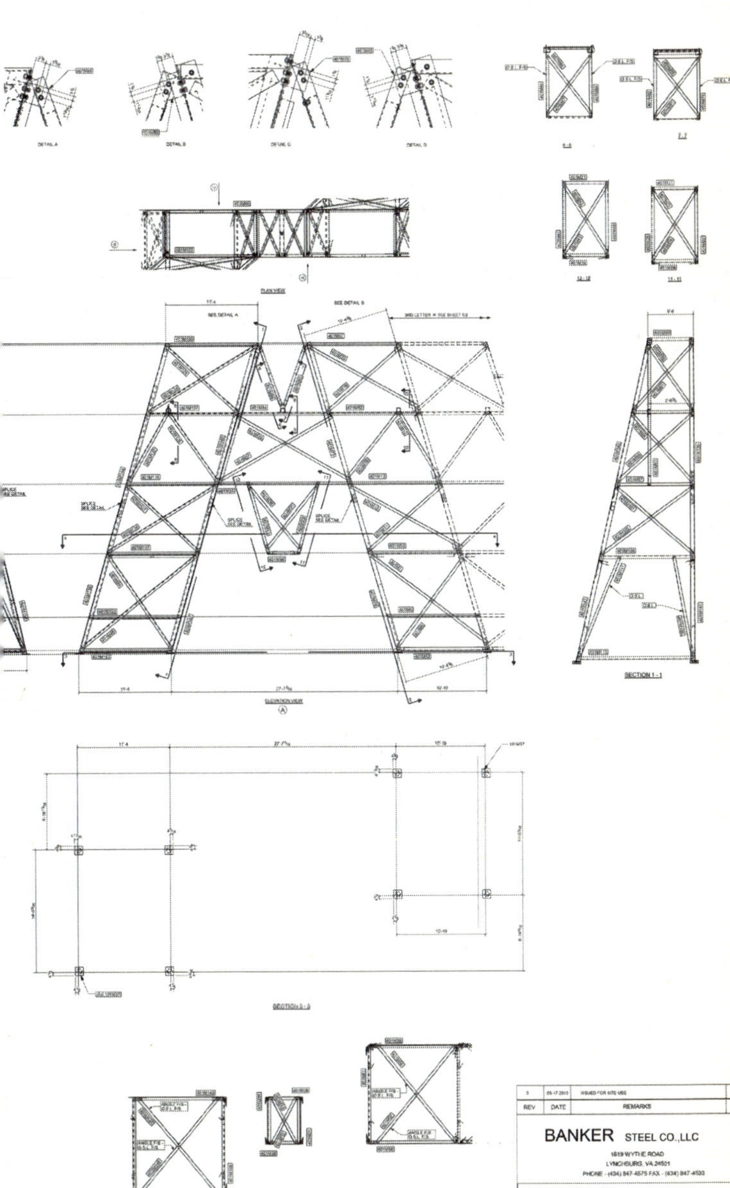

DETAIL A
DETAIL B
DETAIL C
DETAIL D
PLAN VIEW
SEE DETAIL A
SEE DETAIL B
ELEVATION VIEW
SECTION 1 - 1
SECTION 5 - 5
SECTION 4 - 4
REV
DATE
REMARKS
BY
BANKER STEEL CO.,LLC
LYNCHBURG, VA 24501
PHONE - (434) 847-4575 FAX - (434) 847-4533

Hire wire act

Robert Beauchamp

Their challenge became ours as we
detailed the hidden steel structure
under the skateboard skin

close to twenty-two tons later with nearly
five hundred individual shop drawings later
we can say job DONE

still remains to set it up
it looks like a tooth pick model
even in reality but all bolted

a high wire act w/o a net
challenging but satisfying
thank you

for this brain stretching
exercise

we need more

Education is everything

Chris Mills

Absolutely out of the blue they call and said: we have a project. They say it's absolutely nothing that you're used to, but listen. And before too long I say: okay, let's talk tank sizes.

I've been connected to fish forever. I happen to be a fish addict! My degree is in aquaculture (fish farming) and I spend as much of my free time on the coast fishing as possible. My background is building filtration systems for large types of habitats: farmed fish facilities, research facilities, zoos and aquariums etc... I have worked in this field since I graduated from LSU in 1996. My current company specializes in the holding or rearing tanks for the animal life support industries. We also build filtration components but mainly for OEM customers these days. Certain types of filtration applications require specialty resins to resist the corrosive effects of chemicals or harsh environmental conditions. Sometimes we use a corrosive-resistant material liner, but for the most part we just use an FDA-approvable resin, the same material you make a swimming pool or food preparation surface out of. Those types of high grade materials are good for food consumption areas, potable water storage or general human contact.

They say we need this many tanks with this many gallons: one of these, three of these, four of those, and I say you know we build probably four, five hundred different models and well, I can build those for you too, but they'll need custom molds. They think about it for a while and call back and say we don't want to go through that much trouble, so how about we use two of these and three of those which you have, and I say that sounds good. Eventually, they come back and say maybe we'll just use five of the same sized tank, can we do that? I'm trying to fit what I have to what they need, so I say, what about we figure out a borrowing arrangement where I build the tanks, I'll let you use them and when it's all said and done, you send them back.

They sent them back at the conclusion of the project just as they said they would. Basically what they ended up paying for was the shipping round trip, a bit of money, nothing outrageous. We were able to recycle them—one ended up in a public school in New Orleans and another is here in San Antonio at a local school.

We do a lot of work with high schools and community colleges, especially ones in lower-income areas that are working on Ag programs and need equipment but have limited budgets. Aquaculture is a cross-departmental concept. You put together a small system—basically, a fish tank with proper filtration—and you can use it in science class, in history class—the Egyptians used to grow fish forever, back in the day—and obviously chemistry, biology, microbiology because of the biological aspect, physics—even English, with the technical writing aspect— there's a million teaching opportunities and possible uses for these systems and everyone benefits. Plus the kids love playing with fish! They're doing stuff they don't get to do at home. At the end of the school year, they can harvest the fish, they can harvest the plants, and they can have a little fish fry.

Education for our young is everything in this world. I think most of this country's problems would be solved or drastically reduced in a minute if everyone was more educated. Aquaculture in the classroom provides a hands-on trade skill approach to teaching. It is fun and educational for the students. I don't have any reservations about investing in anything that can help make the next generation a little more successful. I have an awesome daughter that I would like to see successful in her coming years. As a parent it is my responsibility to help her and her generation build a foundation for a successful future.

III

The Install

Slight magic

Richard Wilson

All I try to do is magic—but it's not called magic. What's it called, exactly? I guess what I do is give the illusion of something, and do just enough, for long enough, to keep it from falling over, before it's on to the next thing. I am a like an electrolyte molecule. You know, in electrolysis, everything gets covered in gold or whatever. I'm like that liquid, a little module, bouncing back between PS1's directors and building services and whatever the installation is. I'm PS1's practical link to the architect team. You know, the ground here is twelve inches lower than on the other side; the water pipes go here and here, so don't drill too deep here, you know?

Besides the installation, a lot of other things have got to go into the courtyard, and that takes some working out. We have to think about beer tents, signage, sound booth, information... and we have to accommodate the museum operations stuff—like delivering ice to the bars. And think about people lining up: how do they snake through the courtyard? How does that interact with the architecture? Even before *Party Wall* was built, we looked at the platform designs and made adjustments.

It's like another layer of architecture on top of the architecture. There's the structure, but there's also, how to do things in a certain space, the movement of people in any given space. And crowds are a big thing: the Warm Ups on Saturdays host 5000 people from noon until nine o'clock. You're shoulder to shoulder with a whole courtyard of bodies. It's a tidal wave hitting you once a week. Then you have to get it all back together again for Sunday.

The Warm Ups are a huge part of our income in the summer; if we don't get the people in, we don't get cash. And so if you have a structure where people can't get in, or they might hurt themselves—and you go to court, or who knows, anything can happen—then, it's a real-life balance between architectural content and practical reality.

It seems to be getting more and more complicated year after year. Not from the finalists' side, but from our side. We're growing as an institution. Last year Klaus wanted the structure to be able to house discussions, those sorts of things, and CODA came up with the idea of moveable seating and platform areas. There was supposed to be a church in an adjacent courtyard too, and CODA's project made a font that connected the Wall and the church, but that project that never came to fruition. Based on what happened the year before, or what other events and exhibitions we are having, the brief seems to change a little bit every year.

I work in a place where—you know that triangle of quality, money and time? Well here, they never pick just two of the three, they want all the bits of the pie, all the time. People keep saying, pick two, pick two, but not here. In any case you try to squeeze as much as you can out of nothing. You try, for example, to work out the world's cheapest flooring. You try to find paint that is also filler. You try something, anything that cuts out steps, reduces a drying time, alters the laws of the universe a bit, and achieves it without costing a fortune. I spend my time like this. Like just today, I was thinking about how to make a door in this hallway—or more of a partition that folds out, let's say. So I'm thinking: now, do I really need that top bit? And then: do I really need a frame? Then even later: do I really need all those hinges? Anything that cuts down my number of steps. So I spend my time figuring out how to make magic, slight magic.

You turn around, something's not there. You turn around again, boom. A huge installation wasn't there last week, all of a sudden. That's magic too, in a way.

The pain of poor quality far exceeds the pleasure of a lower price

Meinolf Schulte

The problem with foundations for a temporary structure on a site like that is you can get in trouble easily. The size of the *Party Wall* could cause big problems, since there's so many underground utilities there, like water and gas. If you come in with an excavator, digging all kinds of holes, pouring concrete, then three months later you have to come back to dig it back out. You'd completely destroy the surface—and maybe a whole lot more.

The general idea of the ground screw is it's a reusable foundation system. It's pretty straightforward—they can replace any type of concrete footing. Down there in New York, we knew the challenges, we knew the terrain, we knew the soil conditions. We sent our guys down, they put the screws in the ground in the span of a day, handed over the site, came back in three months, took the screws out, and put them back in the warehouse so we could use them again for something completely different. The only thing you leave is a three-inch diameter hole in the ground. You fill it in with some sand or gravel, and no one will ever know you've been there at all.

With this product, I learned that seeing really is believing. You can talk to people about a concept, show it to them, and they might even like it—but until they've seen it put in the ground and they get to pull on it to see how solid it really is, they won't trust it. Actually, I'm the one who brought this product from Germany eight years ago. Now we

manufacture our own screws; we've redesigned and improved the whole concept. But before that, no one had even heard about it over here. Bringing it to the States was an expensive, exhausting process: not too many people understand what it takes to get in front of engineers and officials, to satisfy their requirements, and then start distributing it to the right people. Our biggest market right now is the solar industry, mounting solar arrays. But we also work on highway signs, container houses, house additions, fencing, you name it… it has almost endless applications. *Party Wall* was a small thing for us: twenty screws, each one two meters deep, with the steel structure screwed to the top. But just

imagine building a solar farm: we put up 6,400 foundations for an array project in Massachusetts. With standard concrete foundations, that might take you half a year—we did it in 10 business days.

We believe—*we know*—that the manufacturing and production of concrete is the second largest polluter in the world. With the ground screws, you have a higher-quality and much more sustainable product. You can remove and reuse them, or you can sell the steel back to the scrapyard and get it back into the recycling process. In this industry, they are awesome for their flexibility. It might not appear cheaper up front, but as we tell our clients, the pain of poor quality far exceeds the pleasure of a lower price.

Dumb erectors

Kris Amplo

We were contacted by one of our customers, Banker Steel, a guy by the name of Tom Faraone—he's a good friend.

It's not something we typically get involved in. But it came at a good time in our schedule in the summer, and so we sent over some of our manpower and one of our cranes, erected it from the ground up, and a few weeks later they called us back to take down our wonderful work! Simple.

On our end, we were donating our time and labor. We were paid some of our fees, but mostly it was one for the overall cause, if you will. We employ union guys: they're highly skilled, they've been with us a long time, and they work diligently through all sorts of situations.

Rain impacts us tremendously. It's unsafe to be out there, in the steel, up there in the air. We had to push the schedule a bit, but the guys worked some late hours to make sure we answered the call. Then the rest of the trades, following behind us, could do their thing.

For us this is a very small project. Normally we put up big, heavy structures. Nonetheless we were still challenged, sometimes even more so than some of the frames of real buildings. We had to figure things out in the field.

Here, it's all about finesse. There were several hundred pieces of steel to be put together, everything on angles and with different segments. We put together each of the upside-down letters on the ground, lifted them up on the crane, got the parts on top of each other.

The thing is, when you put up a piece of steel, it's heavy, and gravity takes over. When you put up a column, say, for a building, that column stays relatively plum. When it's about lining up a cross-member, it's basically a matter of putting it all together: they don't bend into each other, there's no flex in the members.

But in this structure, everything flexes into itself. Horizontal members were put at a 45-degree angle, or 33-degree angle.

You put up one letter, and then other letter comes in from the opposite side, and you've gotta frame it with a cross-member, so you've gotta figure out how to keep that one side stable, so you cross-member it to the other side so it all comes together.

We've seen some rather extravagant structures in our line of work, this being one of them. It's much easier to put things down on a piece of paper, but when you get into the field to build it… So there was a lot of trial and error, coming up with methods of how to handle all these pieces, and making them stable enough until the members next to them were erected, so nothing falls over.

We're a labor-only company, we don't make, produce, or design anything—we just erect it. We send the manpower to the field with all the necessary equipment. The saying in our industry is, we're just a dumb erector. But without us, not a thing would go up!

Old New York and new New York

Art Domantay

Caroline came to me in my studio in Greenpoint. Asked if I could do it. Hollwich had sent her to me. An unusual project with unorthodox materials. I could not solve it right away. That's what intrigued me. Made me want to stick with it.

And I said yes. Probably. Because I'd done it before, twice, first for *Public Farm 1* and then partially pre-planning with Eric for *Wendy*, the year before. Then when you don't do it, you miss it. And I did miss it. I wanted to do it again.

It's an impossible amount of pressure for the architects. There is excitement right away and a tremendous amount of fear, because now they know that they have got to make it. The money is small and there's no time. They have to stop normal life. They can't just draw it, they have to go out and build it, but they become better architects through that.

I met Hollwich when he was visiting *PF1*. He told me he'd like to win some day and if he did, then he would want to work with me. And then he did and he did. I suggested Eric's company for the high-up stuff and I guess they took care of the insurance.

My company grows from one to twenty-four installers. It goes from not existing to a massive team that is all handpicked, depending on the project. We put together fifty tons of sugar and five tons of foam for Kara Walker's sphinx in the Domino Sugar Factory. We built Duke Riley's pigeons project. I become an expert in these unusual materials for making artworks and new systems, and then they are rarely used again. My knowledge is shelved.

When I did *PF1* with Work AC, I didn't have a general contractor license. I wasn't insured. It was a handshake between me and the architect and PS1 that we would do our best, that no one would get hurt. That was back in 2008. That was the old New York way of doing it. Over the years, because the projects kept getting bigger and higher, they said all these outside people have to be heavily insured.

Then, in 2013, it turned out to be a different city. Caroline wanted me; preferred me, she said, over the others she ended up with. But in the new system, the new New York, I couldn't do it.

By the following year, I got insurance and I was able to do David Benjamin's *Hy-Fi*. But I didn't build *Party Wall* and I feel sorry about that.

If you're hiring me to do this, you're hiring me to do this

Eric Winston

Coordinating.

Watching.

Scheduling.

Getting everything together.

Planning out the logistics of the day-to-day.

Because my word is the way it goes—or it doesn't happen. Designers design these spectacular pieces that work... in theory. They're great designs, all of them, but they're architects, not engineers. These architects did the smart thing, they went to the guys who won it the year before, and then they were like, just call Eric, just talk to him. If you're hiring me to do this, you're hiring me to do this.

Figuring out how to attach things.

Making sure everything works.

Figuring out the minute details and keeping three steps ahead of everyone else.

Keeping a safe environment so there's no chance of injury.

Because there are the volunteers, too. You have to be able to pretty quickly assess their skills and coordinate their labor. A ton of them showed up all gung-ho, and they wanted to be part of everything from the first day. But at the same time they're still students with very little real-world building experience, and we're dealing with big, heavy structures.

So when I knew I'd be working with fifteen or twenty of them, I was really adamant: this is going to be a pain-in-the-ass bunch of kids who don't

know anything, just standing around! It's going to cause more problems than solutions! But I stand corrected. The quality of the volunteers was high. In large part, it's the reason the project went so well. They were willing to do anything, even in hundred-degree temperatures, and they did it with a smile on their face.

Renting custom equipment.

Getting permits from the city.

Dealing with the anchoring system.

Checking up with the steel company for the structural work, making sure it was going up in the right order in a timely matter...

...Which, unfortunately, it didn't. Because funds are limited. The amount of money is no-

where near what it costs to build it. Honestly, for what's being built out there, it simply could not happen if a majority of it wasn't donated.

We lost almost a week and a half on the steel install because of pouring rain in April and May. They're a union company; if it rains for more than an hour, they go home. It got a little frustrating, but we worked around it, and it was a happy crew on all sides. That's my job—keep everybody happy, keep everybody moving.

When you can't fully control it, that's when it gets really interesting. Plan A turns into Plan B turns into Plan C, and all the while, PS1 is sitting there, thinking, why isn't there a structure going up? What's the problem? You have to get creative and say, we're working on it, you make it look like you're working on it.

Not just the lighting guy

Ryan Paxton

When I first walked onto site, I was the "lighting guy." I did a lot of light-based installations for my BFA at Oregon, and when I came to New York, one of my first jobs was as the shop electrician for Eric at SFDS, who was installing the 2012 PS1 pavilion, *Wendy*. So I worked a bit on that. He liked to take on risky projects and he did it again for *Party Wall*.

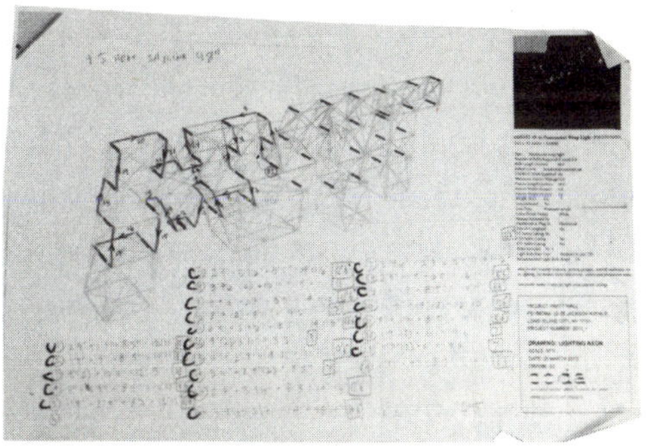

My work began in the basement office at PS1. I had a lighting diagram from CODA, over top of which I had drawn my wiring plan. Caroline measured the distances in Autocad, while I figured out how much wire we needed. It seemed problem-free, but as soon as we went outside to the courtyard, I realized I had been given some wrong information. I had been told that we were attaching LEDs to tube steel, but immediately I saw that these were L-angles. So on that first day, Caroline and I sat there on the PS1 steps, completely rethinking the attachment system. At that point, we both still thought I was the lighting guy.

My boss was insistent on using LED rope lights. I told him, they aren't going to be bright enough—the project called for fluorescent tubes. There's a big difference between a fluorescent tube and an LED rope light. I mean, it's theater lighting, it's not really meant to illuminate. But he guaranteed that they would work. What does it mean, to guarantee something?

We put three- or four-foot sections of rope light on every horizontal member of the structure between the two facades. There were probably two hundred horizontals—whatever it was, it ended up being a lot of these lights. And pretty intricate: we had to run wire from one light to the next throughout the whole structure, tie wires onto wires, and hide it so none of it was slack.

The steel structure was supposed to be completely up by the time I got to the job site, but the union steelworkers fell way behind schedule early on. It had started to rain—and even if it's just barely drizzling, they won't work. We lost a lot of days like that.

But when it came to crunch time, they pushed

through and worked late. There was so much involved in the whole project that we could focus on other parts while they were erecting the last couple letters. I remember times when the steel guys had gone home, it was pouring rain and Richard or Caroline and I were up in the lifts, in raincoats, taping magnets to LED strips.

The last week of the build—less than a week before the opening—we finally stayed until after dark and turned the lights on.

It was a pretty dull glow. No illumination. No lighting, just points of light.

We all sat there in silence.

The next day, Caroline went down to the PS1 shop, got a construction light with a halogen bulb, and put that up in one spot. We tried it again after dark: it worked great. We purchased a bunch of cheap work-lights at Home Depot, and installed them all in a day. Have you seen pictures of the *Party Wall* at night? It was a pretty pleasant surprise. You know that pattern they used in the t-shirts and the towels? That was projected onto the building through the shadows. We had the work lights aimed up at the water bladders, those big, blue udders. It made the whole thing glow. We didn't use a single one of those rope lights in the end.

*

By the end, I had so much more to work on besides the electrical. I was running the job. In particular, I

MoMA PS1

must have spent half my time on site inside one of those water bladders, trying to fix their endless leaking. We worried about them the whole time. Their valves were impossible to seal—and I'm no plumber.

I ended up just epoxying all the fittings together on one of them. It wasn't pretty, but it solved the problem. But we tried many, many solutions before we got to that, including some weird options, like a gelling agent that is used in hospitals to congeal liquid waste.

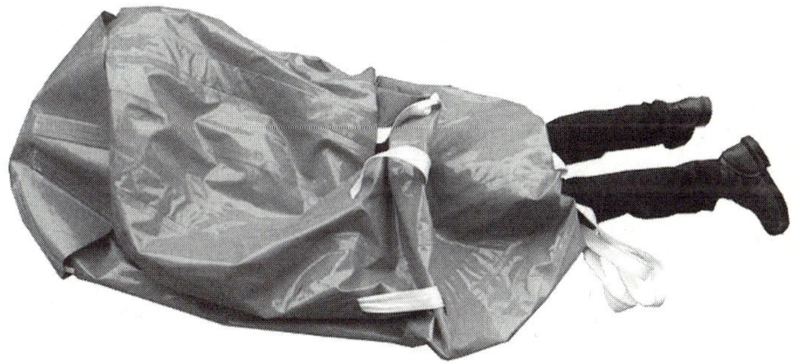

That wasn't even the end of the bladder problems. My boss said we had to fill them with the fire hose from a hydrant. This became a big issue. You have to get a permit through the city, and you have to rent special equipment to pump the water, from the hydrant across the street and into the courtyard. As these bladders kept leaking I would have to drain, refill, check for leaks, repeat, all the time getting new permits.

Eventually I got fed up—I took a garden hose from PS1, threw it in the bladder and turned it on, and went to work on something else. Within an hour it was full, a thousand gallons of water. My boss was not happy that I just used the garden hose instead of doing what he told me.

There were lots of other issues to deal with. When I could, I helped the rest of my team with mounting the facade panels. I also dealt with the aerial water system, which involved another disagreement with my boss about the placement of the water tank. He wanted to paint it blue and hang it as if it was one of the "missing" bladders. We did it, but when Caroline saw it, she said it looked like there had been a horrible accident on the site. I agreed. Finally we were able to relocate the tank and paint it black so it was not so visible. The team joked that I had superpowers: not only could I fly (I was always up and down and all around the site, in my cherry picker), I could also make things invisible.

I was there to make sure that everything was done the way it should be. But I wasn't out there just to make my pay-check. There was more to it. I stood behind this project. I thought it was worthwhile. And I understood its intentions conceptually, so that helped in finding appropriate solutions to problems. And I made sure to see it through, before I quit my job.

Change-ups

Richard Nelson-Chow

I didn't pack a lunch. I hadn't eaten breakfast, but it was a Friday, and raining hard. Surely construction could not happen outdoors today. We might assemble some benches in the attic in the morning, and then Caroline would send us home, where I would crawl under the covers and watch a movie and gradually fall asleep again.

The basement office had a chair and a desk with a computer on it, several large plastic tubs filled with tools, and a couple hundred shrink-wrapped skateboard decks waiting for bench legs to be bolted onto them. Ryan was standing in the middle of the room, right under the light, a giant wearing bright yellow waterproof coveralls. The light reflected off them, amplified by his 6'4" frame, projecting a golden glow, like the bladders did in the renderings.

"It's really coming down today. Gonna be tough, up in the lift."

I took off my jacket, which had not lived up to its "waterproof" promise, and tucked it in a corner next to some Home Depot bags, which were being ripped by their contents and on the verge of falling apart, spilling screws all over the floor. Ryan pulled out a couple of safety harnesses from a plastic tub.

"Hey, so my boss isn't sending anyone else over here today because of the rain but I want to put up some more panels. How would you feel about helping me out? You don't have to if—"

"Yes!"

I had only gone up in the lift once before, but it was by far the most enjoyable activity on the construction site. It was a boom lift: a contraption with four large wheels, a rotating base, and an arm that both telescoped and articulated and could send the basket, which held up to two people, fifty feet in the air. At the top, when fully extended, the view extended beyond the walls of the courtyard into eastern Queens. I put on the harness and went outside.

The massive white canopy was currently sagging under the weight of the morning's continuous rain. A custodian jabbed at the underside of the swollen fabric, trying without success to push rainwater away from the center and over the edge. I looked out at the construction site. The steel workers were long gone. Ryan was waiting for me, and handed me a raincoat that might have been made from the same fabric as his coveralls.

"Ready?"

We walked down the steps into the courtyard and I put up my hood as we left the shelter of the canopy. We were going to be attaching facade panels onto the steel structure, which was almost the length of the courtyard and as tall as the museum.

The process was likely going to take the rest of the month, since each of the hundreds of panels took between five and ten minutes to attach.

Ryan put an armful of tools and hardware into the basket of the lift and climbed in. I turned towards the piles of panels lying on the gravel under blue tarps. Looking down at the crumpled map of the Wall with ink starting to bleed as raindrops hit it, I found the pile that contained the specific panels we were looking for and dragged out the first one. Turning it upright, I staggered towards Ryan. The panels looked light and a little flimsy, but were actually almost too heavy for one person to carry. As I reached the lift, Ryan clamped it on to the side of the basket. I slipped under the railing to join him in the basket, hooked the end of my harness onto the railing, and we started to ascend.

I had seen Ryan every day for the past week and a half since I'd started on site, but I'd never talked to him. On a regular day he had to deal with a variety of people: PS1 employees who were worried that we were disturbing the museum visitors, SFDS workers who looked to him for guidance, and not to mention us—the dozen or so volunteers with no construction experience, whose time had to be productively managed in some way. I leaned back on the railing and looked out as we slowly crept up.

"So where are you from?" he asked.

"From here. New York City. I've lived here all my life. You?"

"Maple Valley, Washington, close to Seattle."

"How many people live there?"

"About 2,000. I can't imagine growing up in New York. It's just so crazy."

"A town that size must be really different. I feel almost the opposite about where I go to school. Ithaca has so much... nature everywhere. I didn't like it at first but the past couple years I've started to enjoy it."

"My favorite thing growing up was being able to just go out and make things. We had a small shop at home and I was always in it. Actually I think that's what led to becoming an artist."

"I didn't realize you're an artist."

"Yeah, this is just a day job. I like building things, so it makes sense."

"What sort of work do you make?"

"I make sculptures involving light. I wire the entire gallery to create specific lighting conditions."

We arrived at the top. Ryan held the panel firmly in his arms.

"Ready?"

"Yes."

"OK, I'm going to unclamp it."

"..."

"Move it over a little. Right. Right some more. Up a little. OK."

I clamped the panel onto the steel and Ryan exhaled. This was the most difficult part, holding the heavy panel forty feet above the ground while making sure it was in exactly the right position to be bolted on. We paused for a minute.

"Actually, my parents are artists too," I said, "My dad's a painter and my mom's a sculptor. Different from your sculptures though. She carves small pieces out of wood and assembles them together."

I grabbed a drill from the floor, bent down, and stuck my arms through the railing, aligning the drill bit with the hole in the beam behind the panel.

Pointing the drill toward me felt strange, but it

was the only way to make sure the holes were lined up. I drilled four holes then stood back up to grab bolts and washers.

"Did you ever play sports?"

"Yeah, I used to play baseball. I got hurt sophomore year in high school though, so I stopped after that. How about you?"

"I did too. I was a pitcher."

"No way, me too. What pitches did you throw?"

"I had a good fastball and slider, but I always wanted to learn the change-up. I feel like it's such an important pitch, but I could never get it."

"Yeah, the change is tough. I only had a fastball and curve."

"Pitching is such a solitary activity. You're out there in the middle of the field, and you have all the time in the world. Everyone's waiting for you, watching you."

"Yeah. Now that you mention it, that's what I like about it. It's not reactionary like most aspects of sports. You get to initiate the action."

"I really miss it."

I looked out, beyond the basket, beyond the courtyard. Many scenes had become visible beyond the walls of the museum. The cars on the Long Island Expressway drove over a tall bridge above Newtown Creek, barely visible in the grey mist. Taxi drivers on break sat under the awning of their depot headquarters, playing cards. The 7 train emerged from the tunnel and rumbled along to the elevated track above a nearby street, pulling into a station. From the confines of the courtyard I looked out, and from the outside some people looked back at the Wall, a sign peering out at the world and signaling.

I tightened the last bolts and we headed down for the next panel. I had forgotten that I was even hungry.

What month is it?

Joon Hyuk Choe

The facade panels arrived in a forty-foot-long truck and were brought in on four palettes, roughly corresponding to the four letters. The two "L" piles were laid down in the main courtyard, adjacent to the already-erected "L" structures, and the "W" and "A" piles were set aside at the other end of the triangular courtyard, where the steel was still in progress.

Michael had come down from Ithaca with the panels, after pushing Comet for more offcuts and weaving skateboard "bones" right up until the last moment. He was coordinating the application of the panels using an elevation drawing where each panel was numbered. He called out a number, and my team sorted through the stack to find the correct panel. Panels had to be applied from the bottom up, since they overlapped vertically. We were able to apply the lowest tier by ladder, but above that, the SFDS "sky team" was mounting the rest using the cherry picker lift.

The application was not always straightforward. Sometimes panels were hard to find, or did not line up correctly. We had to leave gaps for the delayed bladder installation on the third row vertically—they were still leaking and needed constant filling and repair. Jessie arrived and took over panel repairs.

One day, late afternoon, Michael had to leave early for a tetanus shot: he stood on a rusty nail and then kicked the steel in frustration, injuring himself twice. He handed me the by-now crumpled elevation drawing, and asked me to watch over the panel-attaching process for the rest of the day.

Every time there was a question, or an alignment check, I would hear the lift team would shout down to the ground:

"Joon!"

I ran from my job sorting or hanging low-level panels to answer their questions. Apparently, the lift team was satisfied. Michael, swamped with many other jobs to coordinate, was happy to hand off the responsibility: I became the facade man.

Between the construction team and the volunteers, everyone needed information from me. My name the most commonly heard word on site, even more common than "Wall." Over time it became elongated, like several extra "O"s were added, and it was always shouted rather than spoken. Once, over the noise of the diesel engine of the lift, Caroline shouted at me:

"Hey! What month is it?"

I had no choice but to reply.

"Jooooon!"

Moving heavy things around

Zachary Tyler Newton

Out in the courtyard, we were moving and stacking pallets back and forth in the hot sun, and I was thinking, this is fine, I don't mind doing this kind of stuff, but I'd never been very good at moving heavy things around, and I'd been in New York for a little over a year at that point, and had been very ambivalent about what direction I was going with my life, and I just had finished—well not just—but I had recently finished school, and I'd had some freelance projects here and there, and people kept saying to me, oh, you should do photography. I said, you know, I don't mind the hefty labor stuff. But, if you don't have a photographer, would I be able to do that? That's how that took off. Everything's been different since.

T-shirt

Gosia Pawlowska

There are no clothing stores in Long Island City. I know this for a fact, because, while I was sanding down the dance floor, I sweat so much that it soaked right through my volunteer t-shirt.

Needing a solution, I looked all around, but all I could find was a pet supply store. Inside, there was only a dog t-shirt with “I <3 NY” on the front. I bought the large, cut off the sleeves, put it on, and went back to work. Nobody seemed to notice…

Beyond physicality

John Lai

It was my first year at Cornell. Suzanne was my T.A. And I'd been to the summer school two years ago too. Caroline spoke to me; she had spoken to a lot of people. I asked to help. But they were being vague about it.

I never made it to Skateboard Saturdays. And I wasn't on the design team. But I figured out how to be involved. But not. Here and there. And then.

I went to New York. At some point I just decided to. Suzanne said by email, "Actually we don't really need you right now." After a couple days sitting around, I showed up on site. I came with the assumption that I could hop in. "Too many volunteers. And too many doing nothing." I went away.

People sat around. Everyone wasted time. Everyone would do just one thing, and then stand around and watch. Caroline didn't voice her frustration, but I could see it on her brow.

I showed up again. Suzanne said, "Oh, John! You're here." I said, "I know you don't need help, but…" I started helping. I put on a hard hat. I made it there early. I got more and more involved.

Soon, it was Richard [169] and Joon [175] and I who were the core team, running sub-projects. We ended up doing a lot of work. Richard figured out the leaking bladders with Ryan. Joon directed the panel installation. I put up panels. I took it into my own hands. I ended up in the lift.

Brit on site

Shane Pickles

My wife's sister was working on this project in New York and she said, jokingly, if you have nothing to do, you should come and work on it. She did not actually expect me to come from England!

With delays in the steel work, and the student volunteers not allowed to climb the structure, I was the only one permitted to join the steel crew. My experience as an engineer was put to good use. I grabbed a harness and utilised (yes, the English spelling) the hydraulic lift to clamber all over the structure and "snap" all the bolts that the steel workers were installing metresahead of me. From my vantage point, up high, I had an incredible view of the New York skyline, so that was my tourism. Every time I took a moment to have a look around, huge sections of the skin had been attached and the Wall was taking shape with the City behind it. That was the first two days. The next three days were spent attaching the skin panels to the structure, directed by Joon, who made sure we got the right panel in the right spot. I have rarely seen such desire to get a job done, and done right. We got into a good rhythm and cracked on with the task at hand.

Cease work Friday was our cue to adjourn to a local hostelry and partake in a few (using the term extremely loosely) of New York's thirst-

quenchers, where glasses were raised to new friends. The trip also gave me the rare opportunity to spend some time with my brother-in-law, Fergal, who was helping on site that week too. I wanted to stay longer but I was worried that my wife would not like the idea. I made shepherd's pie for my sister-in-law before I left and topped it with the Worcestershire sauce I'd brought from home. She looked like she needed it.

Head of quality

Fergal O'Donnell

I quickly discovered I was out of my element. I had zero exposure to architecture and I didn't have any technical skills: I'd never even worn a construction helmet. So each morning I'd arrive on site with no idea what was going to happen that day, and I would fill in wherever there was a gap. All week I did stuff that I had never done before.

On day one, I worked on the skateboard bone panels. We trimmed and sanded the rough edges, we waterproofed any exposed part where moisture might get in the seams, and we unscrewed and re-positioned a lot of bones that were just not quite right. We'd been instructed how high the quality had to be, so when we had satisfied ourselves that each panel was correct we would move it over into a new 'finished' pile. We got quite an efficient little production line going. Service Delivery: that's what I do in the office. Same concept here, different content. It was hard, hot work, but it was gratifying to watch Pile A diminish and Pile B grow as the shadows lengthened during the day.

Later in the week, I was in the attic at PS1, working with a group to build the skateboard seats.

We drilled holes according to a template and then we attached the legs: some were rubber and some were metal. The metal legs all required sanding to smooth sharp edges. We had a great little team with a positive spirit: some drilled, some sanded, some affixed, and some carried the finished product down the stairs in stacks of three and four.

I'm eight years older than my sister, so most of the other people there were twenty years younger than I am. It gave me hope for the future of mankind to see that kind of generosity: that it's not about the devil dollar, doing everything you can to make a buck—there was no sense of that whatsoever. There was a genuine excitement and enthusiasm, almost as if people were going hiking. All they wanted was to be part of something big.

The right hardware

Mike Babcock

I was working as an assistant district attorney in Brooklyn, but I just wasn't fulfilled. After trying out some other types of legal work, I had this nagging feeling I needed to do something meaningful in my life.

I took Cornell's "Intro to Architecture" Summer Program to consider studying architecture in 2012, and that went pretty well, not least because I met my girlfriend, Vivian [192], who was my instructor there. When I couldn't start university in the fall, I went out to Utah to just live in the mountains for a year. While I was out there, I was thinking: is there something I can do to start networking, to get my feet wet, the summer before starting architectural school? Vivian told me about the PS1 project. I drove back from Utah three days before we were supposed to start—and I'd never met Caroline or Mike or Sue or Joon or anybody really—I just showed up as this random guy off the street, got an apartment in Long Island City.

At first, when we started doing work, we were all just sort of drilling holes in the skateboards, moving a pile over here and then moving it back and then back again—just these organizational things. I didn't really have a clear idea what this *Party Wall* was going to look like in the flesh, how it was going to go up. I mean, who's going to put up the steel? We were all just taking orders.

And then, slowly, roles started to get a little more specific: Joon became the facade guy, John [180] started going up on the cherry picker with Shane [182]. The project I ended up taking ownership of was the benches. I'd done a lot of skateboarding as a kid, and I worked in ski shops putting snowboards together, so I knew a lot about the hardware of connecting things to a skateboard deck.

So I went to the core team and explained the problem of how the skateboards fail. That interaction with them went so much differently than, say, the interaction I had with law partners or judges or prosecutors that I worked for before. Because this time, they were really interested in the right thing being done. No-one on the team was invested in their hardware idea being the hardware that would get used, they just wanted it to be the right hardware, full stop—they didn't care whose idea it was.

When I worked in the prosecutor's office, you could go to your boss and tell them, well, the right thing to do would be to dismiss this case—that's not going to lead them to dismiss the case, because there's politics and other things involved that cause them to go the wrong way. I was attracted to architecture because I felt like it had a little more honesty to it all. I'm sure it has its problems too, of course, but that interaction with the team spoke to me. It made me think, hey, I might be in the right field. People here are really interested in getting things done properly.

I was amazed—Caroline had only known me for a few days at that point, but she gave me her credit card and said, okay, go order the hardware, do whatever you need to do. There were thousands and thousands of these locking nuts with plastic washers in them, the right hardware, and we just got to work.

Caroline's brother, Fergal, showed up and joined my team. He was the hardest worker around. He had his own life and high-powered job up in Connecticut, and he was taking vacation days to come down and work with us, banging out twelve-hour days like a beast.

After we solved the hardware problem, we hit a bigger issue: the original method of attaching the benches to the structure was not working. We went through a lot of ideas. I was riding my bicycle all over Queens to all these metal fabricators, picking up and bringing back different parts, and we would experiment with them. It never seemed to work; at least they would hang the bench on the structure, but they weren't elegant, they weren't effortless, you had to study them to figure out how to put them on. It just wasn't the sort of ease and fun that we would want from people enjoying the project.

I don't know how I had the idea, but, you know, this is a giant steel structure. Why don't we just attach magnets to the skateboards, to the benches?

When I first told Caroline, Mike, and Sue they thought I was joking. But we ordered these 95-pound magnets, three inches wide, and we had to tinker with them, but they ended up working really well. So Caroline said: absolutely, looks great, let's go for it. For the second time I was just completely blown away that I was working with a group of professionals who supported ideas.

By the way, I'm only talking about the good ideas I had—for every good one, I had fifteen really bad ones, too.

Worst volunteer

Vivian Chen

I was working at Morphosis on their Gates Hall project in Ithaca: a graphic scheme for the interior. Rather, I was designing wallpaper. I had never thought about designing wallpaper before this, but now I was developing a whole new appreciation. This 2D graphic can carry engaging meaning underneath the surface, even if it sometimes gets buried beneath this first glance of, *oh*, it's just superficial skin covering a wall. This brought me some insight into CODA's project: you could call it a one-liner, a wall that says WALL (albeit upside-down and inverted), but it embodies much more meaning than that. If you only keep reading.

On my way home from work, I'd stop by to meet Mike [186] on the construction site. I often helped out evenings and weekends, waterproofing the benches and attaching the magnets. There is hard evidence in this in the "making-of" video! But often when I arrived—and this is why some team members say I was the *worst* volunteer—the work was just finishing for the day. They'd just be hanging out or having beers underneath the structure. It was as if my arrival always marked the start of beer-time.

All the tricks

Joe Raia

If you've never been on a skateboard before, you're a little apprehensive at first. It rolls, it wobbles, it's hard to find your balance. You need a practice tool. You need to learn to skate stationarily. You know an ollie?

This Softruck I invented is like a bell curve. They're urethane, just like the wheels, but they're flexible, they don't roll, and you can practice just about anywhere. You get comfortable with the way it moves, you get confident. It allows you to learn a little faster.

Q: Will they really help me skate better?

A: The key to Softrucks is that they help you focus on the mechanics of the trick. As you learn tricks on Softrucks you will learn to position you feet and body over the board. When you are rolling on a standard deck—you will be able to stick those tricks with more confidence!

I don't know if it was a construction guy or a designer or who it was that contacted me, but they had a total understanding of the product. They knew what it was used for, they knew what they wanted it for. They wanted people to come in and use the boards, or use them as benches, all over the place.

Q: Can I do any trick?

A: Absolutely! Any trick that can be done on a regular skateboard can be practiced on Softrucks. While you're at it why not invent a new one?

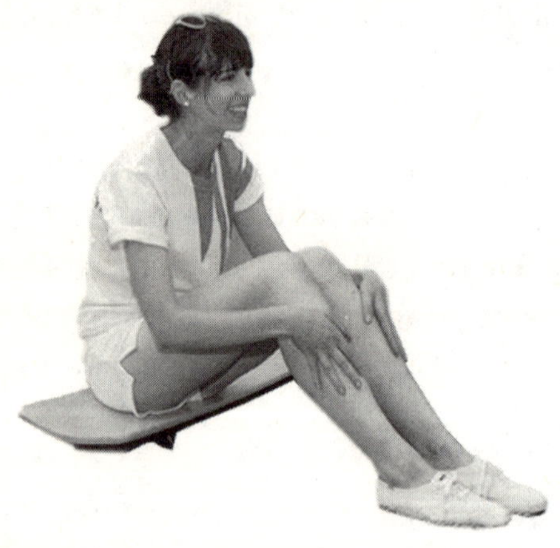

It was a great match. The opportunity the museum gave the *Party Wall* is actually a similar opportunity that the soft truck gives to skateboarders: we give them a temporary space, a practice tool, then you can take that skill out into the world.

We wanted to be involved with something that pushed the envelope. What we do fit their language, the same kind of vernacular and goals, it was mixing the old with the new, the negative space, the secondary and tertiary material uses, the bones and the boards and the trucks.

Q: Will they wear out?

A: Just like your wheels, Softrucks will wear out eventually—but they are designed to take incredible amounts of use. You will have to practice long and hard on Softrucks to wear them out! Fresh Softrucks will ollie higher and have more snap compared to a worn out pair.

The question for me was always: how do you teach a kid to skateboard? One day I had an epiphany. I'm an industrial designer, and so we took these prototypes out into the park, where the kids were, saying, here, try this out—and it was basically instantaneous. Of course they'd be skeptical and say, well, what does this do? And we'd say, it mows the lawn!—I mean no, what do you think it does? It's for what you already do! You already do this.

Now with this product in their hands—or under their feet—instead of going linear, all of a sudden they were going vertical.

Blue

Juliette Joyner

I come in every day at seven in the morning. I start down in the basement, I clean up the shop, sweep up a little in the loading dock, I check the bathrooms and make sure they are clean enough for the public to use. Once everything down there is just about done, I go around the block on the outside of the building. I make sure the pathway is clear for the public to come in. When I am done in the basement, I come up to the first floor, and I'll start on the terrace before I do the actual inside of the building. I do the glass, clean the window sills, sweep the terrace steps, take out the garbage, water the plants. When I do my job, people know I did it. They can tell when I did my job. I try to do my best. I am treated differently because I do a good job.

It was about eight by the time I got to the terrace every day. The supervisor was there and we chatted sometimes. She was coordinating steel workers and telling people where things had to go. The crew came later and a lot of people started doing a lot of things. But early in the morning it was just me and her and the steel guys in the courtyard.

They had a bunch of skateboards and water bags. I didn't expect it to be what it turned out to be. I hadn't seen any models. I didn't know what to expect.

At the last minute, right before they opened it to the public, the supervisor came up to me and asked me what she should use to clean the blue water bags. They had got all kinds of grease and dust on

them that nobody had noticed until everything else got cleaned. I told her to use what we call blue. I gave my spray bottle and a rag. It's like Lysol diluted with a little water. It's like a degreaser type of cleaner. We use it to clean the floors—we just pour it in the water. If you need to wipe down a wall or something, we use the blue. I gave her this blue stuff to clean these giant blue bags.

Yaps

Sixto Figueroa

I came to help a friend in 1997. They had a lot of snow that year. That guy, he talked to me about taking the job. He convinced me. Well, he didn't convince me: I needed it. I was renovating apartments and I needed it. I didn't think I was going to be here for twenty years. I didn't even think I'd be here three.

I've seen every yap. It really doesn't affect my work. My rule is: don't trip the alarm! I am the director of building services and usually what I do is I try to give the yaps what they need: plumbing, water, electrical. They do make some problems. They don't seem to know what bathroom to use. They don't use the basement one: they go to the first floor and dirty the floor. They block the path with trucks so that folks going to the museum have to go around. And there was that bald guy last year who kept parking in the museum courtyard. That guy thought he owned the school.

Each yap is unique. I can't remember the differences anymore, but they all got differences between them. Yap changes every summer and I like change. I think I am looking at my last one this year. It's time to move on.

IV

The Wall

Approach

Susan Rodriguez

Down concrete steps to the train — heading up and out — through the tunnel under the East River — a short journey on a hot evening — expectations build with the rattle of the tracks — bursting out of the tunnel into light — always a jolt — a spatial explosion — revealing the spectacle of the city — moments later the doors slide open — stepping onto the elevated platform into sticky heat — PS1 peeks out of the block below — down steep steps to the sidewalk — a few short blocks to go — what will it be like? — through the entry — a quick right then left then right — a little like Alice through the looking glass — there it stands — commanding the courtyard — how did they make lace out of skateboards? — the light exaggerates the texture — the crowd slowly swells and swarms — inside and out — Caroline speaks — what a NYC night!

*This is not a wall**

Justin Allen

A towering wood and steel wall was erected in MoMA PS1's courtyard where at last Thursday's preview Barry Bergdoll, MoMA Philip Johnson Chief Curator, Department of Architecture and Design, said in his opening remarks that *Party Wall* pushes the Young Architects Program (YAP) to "new heights."

The inauguration marked the "14th birthday" of YAP, the program dedicated to supporting young architects. Pedro Gadanho [253], MoMA Curator, Department of Architecture and Design, reiterated this by saying, "it gives young architects a chance to build." When asked Gadanho why is this important, he responded, "people don't get opportunities often, it speeds up the process." The program and courtyard context allows for more experimental work. "There are a lot of good architects, but these (YAP winners) have that edge," said Gadanho.

How can MoMA PS1 transform their courtyard each year with an innovative perspective in architecture while also providing a new experi-

* Originally published in *DOMUS*, July 2, 2013.

ence for the audiences? Caroline O'Donnell, principal of CODA's winning project *Party Wall* was their answer this year. On the evening of the preview, O'Donnell stated in simple terms, *Party Wall* is a "project about sharing." Linguistically, the project's name makes a clear reference to the architectural term "party wall", a shared wall, to provide common support to two or more parties.

Certain didactics are present that could be applied to contexts outside of the courtyard for different situations and places, where one party does not take a dominant ownership of a space, but rather through coordination, each party becomes a temporary steward of the space altering it for their unique purpose or interest and then returning it back to how it was after use. This is how *Party Wall* functions and this is the beauty of the project.

MoMA PS1's laconic design brief requests shade, water, and seating, this year's proposals were also open to ideas on how to allow programming during the week. O'Donnell and her team were then challenged to create an installation that would be conducive to not only the Saturday Warm Up dance parties but also serve uses for other purposes, including activities organized by CODA as well as the art institution's programming, specifically with *EXPO 1: New York*.

Party Wall accomplishes this best with the creation of four "micro-stages" which produces "flexible experimental space" of undetermined themes available for events such as lectures, film screenings, and performances for up to 300 people. The moveable sitting pieces (made from skateboard blanks) are stored on the lower portion of the wall can easily be taken off and placed where desired in the courtyard, creates spontaneous use and social gathering spaces created by the users themselves, whomever they may be and for what purpose they may have. The sitting pieces are a significant component of the project. It has been demonstrated time and time again the success of having moveable

chairs in public spaces available to its citizens, the courtyard is no different and performs as a quasi-public space to interact with the wall that also enables exchange and encounters.

The form and scale of the project found inspiration from "turning the typical canopy on its side (forming a wall) and creating shade by orienting itself to the southern sun," explains O'Donnell.

"The form of the wall looks like letters. The wall as text or something that you can read has a relationship with its context, i.e., Long Island City's signs, billboards, and graffiti," states O'Donnell. This viewpoint correlates to O'Donnell's work who values writing for her design and research studio.

"We talk about context a lot and what I write really revolves around issues of context and the various ways in which context has been engaged in the past," says O'Donnell.

When asked Gadanho if materiality is more important to architecture today than in previous

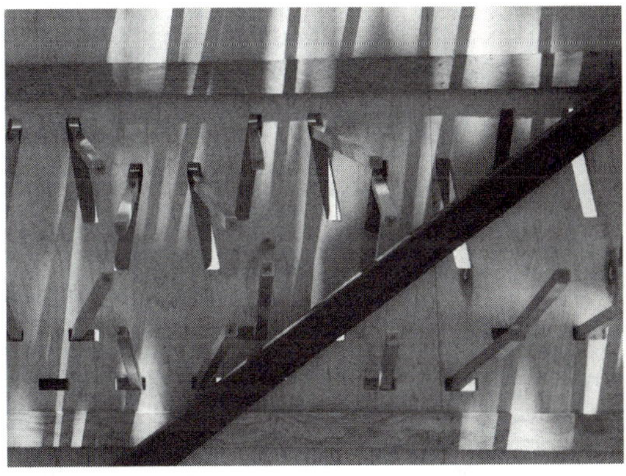

moments, he responded by saying, "yes, but in different ways, now we have more discussions on resources." What better project to involve in the discourse on resources than a project that discusses the sharing of space and material? Each party who uses *Party Wall* has its own interests and yet they complement and balance each other without detracting from one another, but rather enrich.

CODA's research efforts included working with the Cornell Center for Materials Research, who presented a wood byproduct from skateboard manufacturing. 3,000 of these scraps—or "bones"—were used to create 150 panels to make skin of the structure. "We did many studies on weaving patterns because the scale of the cut seemed to us to be too large by itself. Studies were done in Rhino," explains O'Donnell. The structure of the *Party Wall* is comprised of found steel, needing 18 2.43-meter ground screws and the weight of 6 water bladders of coated fabric with PVC coating and polyester base fabric. In addition to the skin and structure, the last remaining element is the landscape itself. O'Donnell explains this best by saying, "I'm not interested in the object, but what is around them."

The project involved the collaboration of a variety of individuals and organizations—Comet for the skateboards, engineers for the steel, MoMA, Cornell University with material research and volunteers, among many others (26 organizations are listed on the *Party Wall* website). When asked O'Donnell what did she learn about collaboration, she responded by stating, "many people are excited to give their time for a project that is challenging, different, and makes their lives and work more meaningful."

There is a hidden message in the project that casts a shadow to spell the word "WALL" in the courtyard, which becomes visually apparent, and is easy to see and comprehend, however the meaningful message is what O'Donnell said and is exemplified in the design, materials, and collaboration, and that's "SHARING."

Architecture

Peter Eisenman

You know why nobody likes this?

They don't?

It's because it's architecture.

Meh

Martin Miller

As an all around hater of most everything, I have often been disappointed by what I have seen from PS1's summer pavilion. When I first saw *Party Wall*, it was through one or another of the many archiporn websites I for some reason feel compelled to check out every so often. Some firm I'd never heard of from upstate. I was underwhelmed. While impressive in scale, it seemed rather singular to me, a simple A-frame structure with a lattice of plywood attached across a rectangular grid.

"Meh..." I thought, "S'alright."

I moved on with my life and forgot about it. Weeks past and I found myself in Long Island City in an apartment whose rooftop happened to overlook the courtyard at PS1. From that vantage point, I could see the structure rising from the space. A shadow was cast across the gravel spelling WALL.

"Hmphhh," I muttered to myself, "That's kind of cool, I guess, I mean I get that, but it's kind of cheesy, right?"

Having nothing better to do one day, I decided to waste some time at PS1. I begrudgingly paid the entry fee to the museum and entered the courtyard.

The frame was impressive in scale and I wondered how they had built something so large with such a small budget. I approached the structure. The plywood panels seemed rather sloppily cut, very rough around the edges and no legible consistency in their irregularity. It seemed a tragic mistake until I noticed a familiar shape in the formed veneer of a nearby bench: it was a skateboard with legs.

Slowly the gears in my head began to turn. I looked at the lattice on the wall, and back to the bench, back to the lattice then back to the bench, lattice, bench, lattice, bench. I extended a single index finger and raised it to my lips, placing my elbow over a folded arm.

"Wait a second..." I said aloud, "Oh my god! These are like totally skateboard offcuts! Like, Oh. My. God! I was totally like thinking they were just like a stupid lattice, but it's like left over from making skateboards!"

The work didn't come to life until I saw it up close. As I navigated the space I found countless clever details incorporated into the work. From every angle I found more and more that I loved the piece. It was clever and witty, active and responsive, it was so much more than a dumb wall.

"That's pretty good," I thought, as I stood admiring the work in the long view, "I'm gonna go get some pancakes."

Ceci n'est pas un mur

Jason Anderson

The familiar that is a little off has a strange and revealing power.

– *Learning from Las Vegas*, 130

In their 1972 book *Learning from Las Vegas*, Denise Scott Brown, Robert Venturi, and Steven Izenour famously coined the terms "duck" and "decorated shed" to differentiate between two approaches to architectural communication: in one, a building is conceived as a sign of itself (a duck); in the other, a relatively more plain building supports and displays an independent sign (a decorated shed). Of course, most buildings are a bit of both, rather than entirely one or the other. But architects like to amuse themselves by arguing over the more apt categorization of this building or that.

So, which is *Party Wall*?

It is a decorated shed. Essentially a scaffold, it is configured to address a given set of functions defined by the PS1 Warm Up program. *Party*

Wall is purpose-built, but in the sense of being provisional, rather than bespoke. It is literally a billboard, endemic to PS1's Long Island City milieu, nestled alongside the Long Island Expressway and not far from the Brooklyn-Queens Expressway. At the same time, it is an architectural folly, a temporary construction that fulfills a utilitarian mission with a certain amount of whimsy, providing shade, a stage, a place to sit, a pool to splash in, a shower under which to cool off. At a distance, however, these functional aspects slip from view, resolving into something like letters: a sign (albeit illegible) draped around a plainly functional assembly.

But it is a duck. While a duck need not be literally biomorphic, *Party Wall* is as animalistic as anything that Las Vegas has to offer. It has an uncanny appearance that calls to mind images of the Trojan Horse. Perhaps there are a few too many appendages reaching down to the ground, but squint your eyes and the likeness is clear. Not fowl, then, but some sort of an ungulate, bent over, searching the gravelly PS1 courtyard for the last bit of grass upon

I AM A
WALL

which to ruminate. Up close, the plywood offcuts lend it a shaggy quality. Irregular, with raw, uneven edges and a coarse surface, the skin is prematurely worn, aged, organic. After spending an afternoon with it, it is difficult to ignore the mild perversity with which the blue ballast bladders have been placed in such a way that they are imbued them with an organ-like appearance, suspended in the chest cavity, dangling between the rear haunches. There is an inescapably visceral dimension to it that can't escape notice.

Both-and. Neither-nor. A sign and a thing in itself. A wall and not a wall. A duck and a decorated shed.

The objects were meant for play

Jonathan Campolo

I knew intuitively what to do with the skateboard "blanks." Even though they had not been milled into their typical and final form and didn't include grip tape, they had the right curvature and were built with recognizable soft-trucks. I could perform any tricks possible with a normal stationary skateboard. Eventually the piece mirrored skating behavior in the streets; as one person started doing tricks, groups flocked to the boards to participate. I saw visitors ollie, pop shuv it, kickflip, heelflip, 360 flip, flatland and more. Over the course of its exhibition, *Party Wall* upheld its parallels to the skating community: because the security staff were perpetually enforcing the "skateboard" objects as seating, they constantly confiscated the boards from people tricking around. This constant policing of the skateboards' use often led to intimidation and—sometimes—confrontation, resulting in a pretty poignant and appropriate reflection on the concept of play. Publicly, skateboarding constantly rides the line

of enforced limitations, making it more fun to get away with whatever you can. The game became convincing both the kids and the authority figures that the objects were meant for play, regardless of age or attitude.

Interaction is liability

Peter Katz

Usually, visitors are not allowed to touch the art in the museum. But with *Party Wall*, the project was not complete until they did interact with it.

It was a great idea. I see that. But for us, the interaction became an issue during the first Warm Up. The music was more mellow than usual. People started taking the skateboards and benches and sat up near the stage. It was interesting on the one hand, but it created an obstacle. Later in the day, we couldn't get enough people near the stage.

It's a real conflict between the architectural vision and reality. In the renderings, people behaved. The benches were out, but neatly. The pools were clean. On Saturdays, in reality, the pools became black by the end of the night. Everything was scattered all over the place. It was a mess. People started to use the low benches as skateboards. I was worried that they would fall and hurt themselves. People were standing on the benches to get a better view. Or dancing on the benches. Some people tried to climb the structure. They always try. But they don't succeed.

I talked to CODA to see if we could not have as many of the benches out during Warm Up. CODA did not especially like it, but agreed to us removing "some." And then, what we thought was "some"

was different from what they thought was "some." CODA would come and see the basement filled with benches and take them back out again. Suffice to say, we had different definitions of the word.

Not in my job description

Anonymous (Security Guard)

I like to work outside in the courtyard and I usually get to do that, because most of the crew, they like to stay inside in the cool. It's not my job to put the benches back in place, but I did it anyway. People would take them out and leave them there and it got messy. I was standing, just watching, which is my job, but it was no trouble to pick up a couple of benches and out them back every so often. It was my way of showing gratitude to the folks who built this, to say thanks for the mister that sprayed a beautiful cool mist into the courtyard in the middle of one of the archways. I stood under it sometimes. I could still see everything and do my job from there. But I was outside and I was cool.

Looking cool being cool

Bryan Roe

Of course we do a lot of boring stuff. Dairies, greenhouses. Look us up—some of it is pretty cut and dried.

But big or small, everything is semi-custom, and the base technology behind these misters is always the same.

I mean sometimes there will be different fog effects, and other times, there'll be a more utilitarian-type purpose: straight-up cooling.

But with this type of thing you really have to look at it from an artistic standpoint. You don't want big pipes showing, right? And the question at the end of the day is, what really is the purpose of it all? Do you want it to look cool? Or do you want it to look cool and, you know, actually be cool, too?

It was summer, and they wanted it to perform. They wanted it to be a real station. First thing they asked was, can we see these misters as part of an aqueduct that alleviates the necessity of a pump?

We said, well… no. Because you know they didn't have a feel for how this stuff really worked. But they had big plans, so we just made sure it was easy to put together.

The heart of our system is a high-pressure pump. It takes a water supply, and pressurizes it to a thousand psi or higher—that's where you can do a real nice dry fog out of it.

We located an equipment room, put a pump there, ran the distribution line—which is just small-format plumbing—and connected it to some high-pressure line that they could work through the thing.

To give it the most visual depth where the fog is deployed we used this four-by-four square stainless steel manifold—that's instead of just a line-shaped manifold—and sat it right there, in this little archway slot underneath the upside-down W.

With our systems, all mist nozzles are usually directed downwards. The designers marked off an area, and after that, all I had to know was: what's going to be below it and, hey, do you care if, say, the ground gets wet? And is it a slip hazard? Is it concrete? Is it tile?

We made it, pretty much like we do it for most every outdoor application, so the evaporation happens before the mist ever has a chance to collect.

We saw it working really well in one photo, it was a wedding, wasn't it? A photo of a party underneath the W. We thought, yeah, that's cool! It looked like they were taking their vows in the mist.

Wedding day

Frank Lettieri

Michael and Sue were engaged in January. Sue made it clear: "No Staten Island Wedding." They had no immediate plans to get married, but there was this competition they were working on, although they hadn't won anything yet. They started thinking, why couldn't we get married there? We could have it for free...

And then they go and win it!

But it was only going to be up for a few months, and it was going to happen in August, so suddenly it's a rush! We had to get everything ready.

Party Wall was just what we were looking for, because the question on all our minds was, after going to all these other weddings, how do you it differently? I mean, the bride and groom would have to come in by helicopter!

The wedding ceremony was at 42nd Street. I didn't even know there was a church on 42nd Street! And who has a wedding on a Wednesday? At 3pm? And then brings everyone across town into Queens at rush hour? It could've been a disaster! It even rained for five minutes, it came down pretty heavy. That would've been bad news if it kept going.

We had a bus drive the guests across town for the reception, from the church to the museum. Sue and Michael suggested on the invitations that anyone who wanted could take the subway or the train, too, but no one did that. The guests were good sports for the most part, but that was one thing too far.

But have you seen the courtyard? With the concrete wall and gravel floor and the sidewalk around the edges—it's ugly. Say there was no *Party Wall*, and someone came up to me and said, let's have a wedding here—no way. Gross! And if we hadn't made it clear to the guests from the beginning, by putting it on the invitations, it would've been an insult! I mean, Can you imagine, if this were a catering hall?: What do you mean there isn't any parking on the streets? And where were the bathrooms? I don't even know to this day!

On the other hand, if it weren't for that Wall, they probably wouldn't even be married. You overlook the gravel, you overlook the bathroom, everything. You make the connection between different worlds, between the families, and of course there's the architecture angle since they built it—and suddenly it's all very reasonable!

Suzanne wanted to invite lots of people, but because of that, she had to divide the guests for supper. On the terrace, there was the first string: family, close friends, and the wedding party. So they go to dinner. Then, the second string comes in! They're set up right by the *Party Wall* itself, and they had someone right there BBQing chicken and corn on the cob. Which everybody told me was pretty tasty.

I have these two other cousins, and it was made clear to them, "You're second string," and they didn't end up coming. I was surprised! Maybe they thought it was like telling them, come to the wedding but grab a pizza on the way. Or maybe it was something else.

In any case, it made it real special. It can't be repeated. It all happened with the absolute minimum of hysteria, which is really saying something if you know my family.

Our house was destroyed during Hurricane Sandy. We weren't even living back in the rebuilt house until April 2013. At that point *Party Wall* wasn't up yet, but the bridal shower was the first event in our new home.

It makes me realize now: *Party Wall* was temporary, it didn't last forever, and neither will the new house. The state is buying out the whole neighborhood altogether, acres and acres, house and houses. It wasn't clear they'd do it at the time, but then 90% of the neighborhood residents insisted upon it. Right afterwards there were some people who weren't going to wait around, and they built new places, like us. So they're brand new, and now—now they're going to knock them back down. Temporary. We're going to do ours in a couple weeks.

After the hurricane people really had no spirit, everyone was really down. Then one hysterical person got them at their weakest point, and started the rush to demand the buyout. No-one wanted to hear about anything else, no compromising. I never saw the government work so fast in my entire life! This is New York City, you'd think mobilizing the buyout would take a little longer, but here we are, it's all happening within a year.

It was the fastest year of my life.

A year of structures going up and down, some of it pretty gloomy. But you have got to remember that while all this is going on, there's the *Party Wall* thing, there in the background, and we were all very much into that. It took the edge off Sandy.

If they'd build a levee like other places up the coast, of course we'd stay. But all around us in Oakwood Beach, you had people who had caught "buyout fever." It's not a huge area, only three blocks, but it's well-defined from other neighborhoods. They're going to plant trees here, make it parklands. We've been here since 1987, and there's been one other major flood, in 1992, six feet, it was a big hassle. Sandy—that was twelve feet!

Right now there's this one guy who operates the machine that takes the houses down. I've been watching his work. He's an artist. He compacts all the materials into a really nice pile of garbage, and then they take it away one by one in trucks. Effortless. I saw him the other day on break and told him, "You know, you're an artist!" And looks at me he says, "Yeah, well, I hate messes." After he's done, there's nothing left in the streets. When he's done, you never knew there was a house there at all.

M. Wells

Sarah Obraitis

We heard rumors that two of the architects, Suzanne and Michael, were getting married at MoMA PS1. We knew the museum's courtyard would make a fantastic backdrop, unlike any other in New York City, but considering the good energy of a new design project, the towering *Party Wall*, and what could be a better start to the rest of your life?

By the time construction was completed and opening ceremonies were being held, we got to know Caroline, Suzanne, and Michael a little bit. They were very friendly but kept focus and kept going. We enjoyed watching them work and more interesting was watching them eat and drink. It was the first summer since we had reset M. Wells after closing our popular diner nearby. At M. Wells Dinette we continued to shuck oysters, make big complex dishes, bring in whole goats and would offer other such ideas. To some visitors, we're just an unexpected kind of cafeteria, but the *Party Wall* crew turned our spot into a clubhouse of great meaning to us. When we see the lunch meeting or the early afternoon aperitif, we remember the early days of the power lunch at M. Wells.

When the creators left their work site at the start of the season, M. Wells had the challenge of welcoming and feeding thousands of music revelers every Saturday. We would move our kitchen outside and make fast fare and serve tanks of cocktails. Needless to say, the wedding planning, which I might have been dreading otherwise, was a welcome respite, and the big fête began taking shape so beautifully. The menu would include roast beef and big fish with loads of sides and a grill that was fired up at 10pm for the 75 additional guests who showed up to the *Party Wall*—a most whimsical, sincere, and accurate name.

Auntie impossible

Tara O'Donnell

One day, my parents and I traveled to the city to have brunch with my Aunt Caroline. During the meal, my Auntie said it might be impossible to build the *Party Wall*. So she wasn't sure that she wanted to win the competition. I asked her why would she not want to win. I mean: who wouldn't want to win something?

In the end, it was almost like a playground. You could play in the pools and do tricks on the skateboards. It turned not to be impossible after all.

You wake up early

David Salomon

You wake up early, make coffee, shower. With you and the car fueled and ready to go you barely wake your girls and guide them towards the back seat. Three hours later, aside the highway, they arise for the second time that day. An hour after that you find yourself staring up into a bright abyss and your brain is having trouble adjusting to the space that appears and disappears before your eyes. Some of you are intoxicated by this effect, others are bored. No bother, you've gotten a great parking spot right across the street. After a knish and a peek at the park you head to your next stop.

You find yourself in front of your father's old place of business right next to the tunnel. You worked summers here in high school and college. The building isn't there anymore, the warehouse has been replaced by a six-story apartment building. Despite some radial changes nearby, the neighborhood still feels familiar. The juxtaposition of light industrial and residential buildings seems as random as it ever did. You tell your girls this. They seem interested but don't ask questions.

You steer the car towards its next destination. It's just down the block. Twenty-five years ago you knew it as the big red building across the street from the post office. That was before you became interested in architecture and art. Parking is surprisingly difficult. Looking for a spot you realize that despite its reputation and affiliation, the institution you're headed for certainly didn't gentrify the neighborhood overnight; which no doubt contributes to its charm. Still, there are signs that things are headed in that direction.

It's a bright but surprisingly cool summer day. You remark how earlier in the summer you had to strategically walk on the side of the street with shade to make things bearable. This is a nostalgic reference to a just-completed trip. It is also foreshadowing: one of the functions of the thing you have come to see is the abatement of light and heat.

We enter the site. It's unclear—literally and ethically—if we need to pay for admission. We don't. You tell your girls that you haven't been here in quite some time. The last visit was with a different female family member. That was also on a Sunday. You didn't pay then either. You were overdressed. It was hot. The installation was cool. You were killing time. You were on your way to a Sunday afternoon wedding. Parking was easier then.

Your other experience with this space was as an "advisor" to a friend's proposal for the same event. It was a heady, optimistic time. It was a good proposal, managing heat through water and organizing program through patterns. It didn't win.

You had some experience with the current project as well. A different friend was responsible for it and you had monitored its progress. A few months back you and your eldest even helped out. It was for her, you said, that you were making this trip for. This was true, but not all of it. You also needed to see the thing finished. You needed to know for yourself. You also wanted to show to yourself and your friend that you made the effort to see it. It was a sign of support. This is also true, but there were other reasons you came this far. You also wanted to see that vanishing space, and to see your cousin and to eat some good food. So did your youngest daughter—that's the only reason she came.

Immediately upon entry you spot a couple you know who were integral to the project you're here to see and which looms above them. That day, the last day it will be on display, they are trying to move some merchandise.

The banter is fun. You really like this couple. They were actually married here just a few weeks before. This thing would forever be a major part of their lives. It's not clear what significance it will play in your or your daughters' lives, but you never know.

The couple chat-up some customers and you and your girls walk around. Although big, there is plenty of room to walk around it in the courtyard. You are impressed with the opacity of the thing but also with its lightness. The pattern is of a high quality. You should know, you are an expert on such things. You and your daughter fondly remember one of the people who helped create it. You are surprised at the amount of shado it produces. It seems to work as intended. The couple confirms this for you. Everybody in your party is enthralled.

You observe the different degrees of weathering on it. You are told it is an index of atmospheric conditions. You wonder what would happen if it stayed up longer. How long would it take to be a ruin? Will it be reinstalled? You find out that it would be very expensive to do so. It's cheaper to literally chop it down. So much for modernism.

There are a few people milling around. There are a few more inside the building. Some of you are entertained by what you find there, others not so much.

You return to the thing and the couple, whose status you tell yourself has gone from being former students to simply friends. You wonder if they feel the same. You negotiate with them an arrangement that will allow you to own a piece of the wall. However, it is unclear as to how you will be able to retrieve it. We discuss a scenario. You leave optimistic but you don't follow up and the chance of owning a piece of it is lost. You lament this often in the future. You don't buy a bench either. Your eldest does pick out a really cool t-shirt. It turns out they don't have her size, but there are some in a box back in her hometown. You pay your money and work out an arrangement. You figure it will be a good excuse to see your friend and congratulate her personally when she returns from abroad.

Your next stop is a touristy restaurant across the river. It takes a little while, but you get a good spot. You started coming here before it was so touristy. Oh well. Anyhow, you've been a tourist in this town for many years now. The food is still good and everybody loves it. You meet a dear relative and her family there. Your eldest ends up walking home with her cousin through the Village. It's great to see her so at ease in the city. These two don't see each other often but it doesn't seem like it. You remark it was the same with you and your cousin. She replies it was the same with our parents, in the same city, six decades ago. You drive uptown to meet them. You find a spot right outside their apartment.

You linger a little longer than you had planned. You recount the amazing things you saw and did in just a few hours. The city seems more magical than ever; more personal too. You must thank your friend for giving you a reason to spend the day with your girls and to add to your family's history. That's what great architecture and friends do for one another.

On the way out of town you grab a big coffee and the girls settle into their pillows. It takes a while to get through the tunnel. It's going to be a very late night. But it doesn't matter, you've got a story you can tell for the rest of your life and there's a good spot waiting for you in the driveway back home.

Circular economies

Jason Salfi

When *Party Wall* was completed, there was a media frenzy. Article after article described Comet's contribution to the project as "a porous skin made of woven skateboard scraps" ("CODA's Skateboard Scrap 'Party Wall' Kickstarts MoMA's Summer Music Series," *ArchDaily*, 2 July 2013, by Karissa Rosenfield), and "offcuts from a skateboard manufacturer" ("Party Wall by CODA at MoMA PS1," *Dezeen*, 2 July 2013, by Amy Frearson). And while these descriptions make it sound easy to harvest our "bones," in fact, it takes considerable effort to care for and store what is normally considered waste. Our staff collected four thousand such pieces over the course of three months. Normally, this material was our heat source during the winter. This year we had to devise a new way to heat the facility. Additionally, since our bones now had a purpose, they needed to be treated like a separate product: they were prepped and clear-coated so they would last outdoors for several months. This doubled the workload for an already hardworking crew. But more importantly for us, this project was a way to shine a light on the possibilities of upcycling materials. Art always has a way of starting a dialogue.

At one point, however, an article came out that was not so positive. The author considered our sustainably harvested natural wood "bland" and seemed surprised that the warm-up party-goers, who were "wandering laconically around, scarcely glancing up at the architectural intervention," were more interested in beer than architecture ("Coda Party Wall at MoMA PS1: Is 'Party Wall' at MoMA PS1 too much party and not enough wall?" *Architect*, July 26, 2013, by Michelle Dean).

While the piece seemed to be a rather desperate attempt at negative criticism, I'm no architect, so I kept reading. But as I read on, I was pretty shocked to read that our project was described as wasteful, erroneously claiming that "the skateboard pieces were from California and that the energy used in travel cancelled out the sustainability of the reuse of material." Now as a professional, I appreciate critique. But in this case I had to defend our sustainability-focused work—that we had not made skateboards in San Francisco since 2007. Or as I described it in my letter to that magazine: "I reckon you could update your facts on where CODA sourced their materials. 100% Ithaca, NY on the wood cuz." Our move to Ithaca allowed us to be closer to our suppliers of veneer, glue, clear-coat, and ink.

I finished my letter with some skateboarding wisdom: "Have a great day. Hit me up if you need a longboard. And remember it's a lot easier to tear stuff down than it is to build it up."

Subsequent to the CODA project, Comet switched back to saving valuable pieces of offcut. Our work with *Party Wall* inspired us to work with other skateboard factories on what could be done at a greater scale. And in 2015, Comet launched the UPCYCLE line as a result. This collection of skateboards is made from 100% scrap that is spliced together. If techniques from this process were deployed at a large scale, the skateboard industry—now the *largest consumer* of maple trees in the world—could collectively use 10% less maple. Comet's goal with this project is to advance dialogue on the material steps that can be taken to activate a circular economy. I encourage journalists to contact me about it, and I continue to be open to discussion. — jason@cometskateboards.com

Case study

Florencia Rausch

As instructors of a first-year design studio at the University Torcuato Di Tella, Buenos Aires, we chose several built works through which students could learn about structures, materials, and most importantly, the impact objects have on public spaces.

In Buenos Aires the street is the place where inhabitants meet, but the concept of the street as a public space is not on the government's agenda. This very absence became a core issue in our teaching strategy: how can we intensify the co-habitation of different social actors in a certain location?

First, we analyzed the area with an analytical-empirical view on public space and mobility. Then, we chose case studies with the aim of extracting key concepts. Student teams explored eight projects: VMX's Bicycle Storage (Amsterdam, 2001), DaF's entrance stairs for the Architecture Biennale (Rotterdam, 2005), NL's Das Netz (Berlin, 2006), Jan Gehl's Broadway project (New York, 2009), West 8's twisted bridge (Vlaardingen, 2009), BIG/Topotek1/Superflex's Superkilen Park (Copenhagen, 2012), and CODA's *Party Wall*. Their goal was to produce a proposal in response to their given site.

One team (S. Baldini, P. Conforti, I. Fischer, V. Pavesi, T. Pierdominici) combed through each of *Party Wall*'s layers. They discovered how water wove through the structure, how cladding was made from the offcuts of skateboards; how you could remove parts of the cladding and use them as seating, re-programming the space. How the Wall unified the incongruous spaces of PS1's oddly shaped courtyard, at the same time enabling different kinds of encounters. How it provoked people

to use the space in countless ways. How you could read the word "wall" in the shadow.

In the end the team designed a project in an existing park that had a neglected wall along one side. They devised an urban infrastructure along it, giving the site new uses, and creating intimate spaces for spontaneous social gathering: sitting, lounging, climbing, shade. Their project, like its case study, also became a billboard for itself: a sign with an effect at the civic scale.

Architecture activating awareness: a postscript on MoMA's Young Architects Program *

Pedro Gadanho

For more than fifteen years now, a full-size architectural environment has been built every summer in the courtyard of MoMA PS1, in Queens, New York, as part of the museum's celebrated Warm Up music series. Each year, the architectural projects were the outcome of a competition for young architects—a program organized by the Museum of Modern Art, which has itself become influential in the architecture field. Now, as the Young Architects Program (YAP) reaches full teenage status, as it expands through a growing number of international partnerships, and as it is replicated elsewhere by other institutions, it is a good moment to offer a reflection on its value—and on what YAP is delivering to the architecture arena beyond a joyful party setting.

As it goes with MoMA's program, every year a pool of nominators identifies upcoming young architects in the United States, a jury then selects five finalists, and lastly a winning team designs and

* Revised version of a text originally published as "Yappity Yap: Architecture Activates Culture, Culture Activates Architecture," in *DAMn* Magazine #43, March 2014, Ghent/Berlin.

builds an architectural installation that activates the museum's patios for different uses. The most enduring of these uses has been to offer a lively background for the Warm Up Sessions—a cutting edge music program that brings a crowd of circa five thousand youngsters to the museum on steamy Saturday afternoons. With the original intention of providing an urban beach to those who couldn't afford to leave New York City during its hot summers, the YAP competition has asked for architectural

structures that could provide shadow, water features, and seating areas. But young architects have always come back with lots more, from water cathedrals to pop-up urban farms.

Over time, new themes have come to nourish the architoctural concepts on display at MoMA PS1's external spaces. On account of architect's inputs, and a competition brief increasingly directed at themes of ecological sustainability, the YAP installations started to inevitably reflect changing mindsets around us. They started to reveal the concerns of younger architects—and how their imagination and ingenuity is put to work to make such concerns palpable. The competition became an architectural showcase on its own. The architecture grew beyond the interactive structure that, alongside the powerful magnet of music, fostered for an atypical museum attendance—the type of audience that may otherwise not have stepped into a contemporary art museum. Indeed, YAP became a barometer of tendencies, and a rite of passage for younger architects in search of a spotlight.

Considering the architectural context in the United States today, one may immediately grasp how YAP and similar programs have become crucial to nurture upcoming talent. The promise of architectural creativity instilled by forward-thinking architecture schools increasingly clashes with the dumb reality of a design market dominated by corporate pragmatism. As hyper-regulation and the terror of liability take over construction, it becomes gradually harder for younger practices to advance and sustain an experimental approach to the profession. If for architects breakthroughs typically come late, it was never so problematic to enter a full practice mode on independent terms as now in the United States. Cultural happenings that allow younger architects to experiment with actual building, while simultaneously offering them visibility on a wider context, become astonishingly relevant.

If one is to measure success through a given program's output, as one usually does in a result-driven milieu, one can only appreciate YAP's enviable track record. If the architectural context provided for the competition's significance, YAP has also built its credits on solid grounds. Earlier winners of the program, such as SHoP, have gone to build outstanding architectural interventions in New York. This is the case of the Barclays Center in Brooklyn, which, polemic as it may have been, has also been voted by many in NYC as 2013 building of the year. On the other hand, more recent finalists, such as SO-IL and MOS Architects, are now part of the rarified young sect in town that have retained an experimental brink as they progressed towards their first international commissions, such as SO-IL's [46] Kujke Gallery in Korea, or MOS' Lali Gurans Orphanage in Nepal.

As YAP's brief came to include requests for a reflection on issues of ecology and sustainability, the program also stimulated a specific creativity and research mode, with innovative answers for clamoring problems. Architects have sought solutions that are simultaneously fun to use, architecturally provocative and jam-packed with clues on how future strategies for sustainability can be re-imagined. This was the value of HWKN's pollution-eating *Wendy* in 2012, The Living's DIY organic brick structure in 2014, or Andrés Jaque's water-purifying architectural device in 2015. CODA's 2013 skateboard-waste recycling *Party Wall* was another great example of how younger architects are able to bring together research and resourcefulness, so as to layer several pressing concerns into one architectural prototype. In this case, CODA allied the need for local sourcing with the upcycling of unexpected materials, making the project not only a 'fun feature' or the site of a dialogue with important past architectural references, but also a construction that conveyed a relevant economic and political concept.

The significance of organizations like YAP, whatever and wherever they may be, lies in the fact that, through media impact and direct experience, they offer a platform and a springboard to make bright architects and their ideas understandable to new audiences. The cultural arena in which these programs take place thus becomes the counterpart to a market that tends towards boring homogenization and economic exclusion. In such programs lies a responsibility that the proposals are not exclusively evaluated for their inherent architectural or spatial qualities, or that the participating architects are not only judged for their potential to thrive in the architectural field. Thus, these are competitions that must support practices with an ability to contribute ideas and new critical perspectives to a broader social discourse. Through such competitions—and beyond the possibility to actually build-up their own portfolio—architects find the opportunity to reach out for audiences and clients that may be attracted to new ideas or out-of-the-box attitudes. A world in crisis needs disrupting responses to actual problems.

The writing of the Wall

Cynthia Davidson

I never saw the wall at PS1. I didn't need to. The wall and its construction, its materiality and its "sustainable practices" didn't interest me; its physical presence—a centerpiece for weekend "Warm Up" parties—did not interest me. But its concept: that interested me. The concept of a wall, of a "party wall" freestanding within the fortifying concrete walls that enclose the MoMA PS1 courtyard; the concept of the word "wall" pretending to be a wall, pretending to be something architectural, these ideas interested me. And because a word, like these words, can be seen on a page in a book or on a screen on my desk, there was no need to make the pilgrimage to Queens to see it.

Before the word was manifest, I did make a pilgrimage to Ithaca, to a vast, cold garage where CODA and a few Cornell architecture students were collecting and sizing the plywood remains of skateboard production that would be used to give the concept materiality. And another pilgrimage to a basement room in Sibley Hall, the school of architecture at Cornell, where mock-ups of various details, like the benches one could pull off the final object, were being tested. I did the due diligence. Talked to the architects. Asked questions. But I didn't go to Queens that summer. Instead, I thought about walls.

And if you think about walls long enough, if you start with Alberti, move through Ruskin, arrive at Venturi and Scott Brown, take a detour through Vito Acconci, the wall as a thing simply dematerializes right before your eyes. In that sense, the next logical step is those supertall recyclable leaning letters, W-A-L-L, upside-down and backwards. Traditionally, historically, a wall separates; it is architecture's great divider, largely used indiscriminately to keep some in and others out, like the PS1 courtyard walls. CODA's word-wall separates itself, splitting into a rough approximation of an A-frame structure and inviting visitors inside. Does that make it two walls defining a space? Denise Scott Brown, in her 1971 essay "Learning from Pop," said that "space is not the most important constituent of suburban form. Communication across space is more important."[1] W-A-L-L, which in its construction bears a strong resemblance to billboards, clearly learns from pop, if not from Las Vegas. But what do we learn about architecture from it? Does it say anything about architecture?

INTERNATIONAL

In his six elements of building—"locality, area, compartition, wall, roof, opening"—Alberti defines the wall as "all that structure which rises from the ground upward in order to support the weight of the roof, or which acts as a screen to provide privacy for the interior volumes of a building."[2] Ruskin, in *The Stones of Venice*, memorably calls the wall the "Wittiest Partition," though he offers no witty definition or description of the wall, and would be hard-pressed to define W-A-L-L as a wall at all. "In perfect architecture ... walls are generally kept of moderate thickness, and strengthened by piers or buttresses; and the part of the wall between these, being generally intended only to secure privacy, or keep out the slighter forces of weather, may be called a Wall Veil."[3]

Party Wall is not solid; it rises up but supports nothing but itself; and while perhaps a "witty" partition, it offers neither protection from weather nor privacy. W-A-L-L is instead an interactive screen, a contemporary "veil" free of a wall's typical programmatic encumbrances.

The actual fact of a party wall, that shared partition that separates row houses or apartments and blinds one to the activity on the other side, offers no transparency, no accessibility. This party wall is at the heart of Vito Acconci's 1977 piece, *The Gangster Sister from Chicago*, an installation of five parallel walls, audio tape, and speakers. Walking in the narrow spaces between the walls, one hears the voices "next door," but sees nothing. The walls constrict space and movement and vision; they visually separate yet they communicate. There is something "beyond" the partitions.

Not having walked between the W-A-L-Ls of CODA's *Party Wall*, I do not know how it functioned, but like its materiality, its temporary function also does not interest me. I am more amused by the concept of the W-A-L-L and the message it sends: it communicates "wall" but there is no physical wall. In other words, there is only a sign, à la Scott Brown, of the times: the writing of the wall.

1 Denise Scott Brown, "Learning from Pop," in *Architecture Theory since 1968*, ed. K. Michael Hays (Cambridge: MIT Press, 1998), 64. First published *Casabella*, December 1971.

2 Alberti, *De re aedificatoria*, 8.

3 John Ruskin, *The Stones of Venice*, 46.

Back Matter

Contributors

JUSTIN ALLEN was a writer for Domus in 2013. He is currently an artist and Director of Spaces Objects Art.

KRIS AMPLO is Vice President of JC Steel.

JASON ANDERSON was an architect at Skidmore, Owings & Merrill in 2013. He still is.

MIKE BABCOCK took time off from practicing law to explore a new career in architecture in 2012. He graduated with a Master of Architecture from Cornell University in December 2016.

ROBERT BEAUCHAMP was Director of Datadraft, a Canadian company who detailed *Party Wall*'s steel structure pro bono. When he was asked, "Why are you doing all of this for us?" he answered: "For art!" It was this positive spirit that often kept us going throughout the project. Robert died in 2016 but his memory and spirit lives on with all of us.

KLAUS BIESENBACH is Director of MoMA PS1, and Chief Curator at Large at MoMA.

JONATHAN CAMPOLO is a multimedia artist and musician currently living and working in Brooklyn, New York. In 2013, Jonathan was a docent at MoMA PS1. He currently works as an archivist at *Artforum* and under Jenny Holzer in studio.

NICHOLAS CASSAB-GHETA was a fourth-year B.Arch student in 2013 and is now an accomplished designer. He has just completed his MS in Computer Graphics at Cornell University.

KELLY CHAN is a writer living in New York. In 2013, she covered architecture and design news for ArtInfo.com.

VIVIAN CHEN was working at Morphosis in New York City

in 2013. She has since taught design studios at Cornell University, and is currently working at Weiss/Manfredi.

Steven Chodoriwsky is an artist, designer, and writer. He is the 2016-17 Peter Reyner Banham Fellow and Visiting Assistant Professor at the University at Buffalo. In 2013 he was a Visiting Critic at Cornell, co-teaching with Yoshiharu Tsukamoto of Atelier Bow-Wow.

Joon Hyuk Choe was a recent graduate from Cornell University in 2013. He is currently a junior designer at MdeAS Architects.

Pippo Ciorra is Senior Curator of MAXXI Architettura in Rome. He curates the Italian branch of YAP, the MoMA PS1 international program for young architects.

Stephen Clipp was the head of facade design and fabrication for *Party Wall* and a Visiting Critic at Cornell University in 2013. He is currently a Lead Design Architect at R&A Design in Los Angeles.

CODA is an architectural firm specializing in site-responsive design and material innovation. Based in Ithaca since 2008, CODA works at a range of scales, from the city to the dwelling.

Cynthia Davidson is a friend and critic who occasionally volunteers psychological counseling.

Art Domantay was installing outdoor artworks for Public Art Fund and Creative Time in 2013. He recently installed Taryn Simon's 350-ton concrete towers at the Park Avenue Armory.

Peter Eisenman is an architect, educator, and theorist.

Emeco make chairs. In America. Often by hand. Mostly from recycled stuff. But always to last.

Sixto Figueroa was the Director of Building Services at MoMA PS1. He retired in 2014.

Nathan Friedman was a master's student at MIT in 2013. He is currently a founding principal of Departamento del Distrito and Adjunct Professor of Architecture at Universidad Iberoamericana.

Pedro Gadanho is Director of MAAT, the Museum of Art, Architecture and Technology, in Lisbon. Previously he was a Curator of Contemporary

Architecture at the Museum of Modern Art in New York.

James Garland, an architect with a thirty-year specialization in water design, acquired his Masters degree from UCLA, interned under Charles W. Moore at Urban Innovations Group, and founded Fluidity in 2002.

Patrick Govang is a serial entrepreneur, mentor, coach, teacher, and executive. He founded e2e Materials, which developed an alternative to wood composites using soy and waste agricultural fibers. He is a past Chairman of Comet Skateboards, a founding B-Corp.

Matthias Hollwich is a partner at Hollwich Kushner, winners of the 2012 MoMA PS1 Young Architects Program where they built *Wendy*, and a co-founder of Architizer.com.

Scott Hughes is a Principal with Silman, a guest lecturer for the Cornell AAP in NYC program, and a proud father of a one-year-old daughter.

Florian Idenburg is an architect in New York, founder of SO–IL (winner of YAP 2010), and Professor in Practice at Harvard GSD.

Michael Jefferson was the co-project Leader for *Party Wall* and a Visiting Critic at Cornell University. He is currently a Lecturer at the University of Michigan and Co-Principal of Je-Le.

Juliette Joyner is a Maintenance Technician at MoMA PS1.

Peter Katz was Chief Operating Officer at MoMA PS1 from 2011 to 2015. He is currently Executive Director of the Reversible Destiny Foundation, an artist foundation created by Arakawa and Madeline Gins.

Joe Kennedy was a student in the B.Arch program at Cornell University in 2013. He is currently pursuing a Fulbright research grant at the Oslo School of Architecture and Design.

Ben Kessler was studying architecture at Cornell in 2013. He graduated in 2016.

Kent Kleinman is the Gale and Ira Drukier Dean in the College of Architecture, Art and Planning at Cornell University.

Bryan Kramer is Vice President at Extra Packaging LLC.

Jerry Lai was AAP Visualization Support at Cornell in 2013. He is currently an architectural designer at Marvel Architects.

John Lai had just completed the first year of his B.Arch degree at Cornell when he worked on site. He has continued to work as part of CODA since then, taking a lead on the *Urchin* pavilion in 2015. He is now taking a year out with Barkow Leibinger in Berlin, and plans to complete his degree in 2018.

Alexis Lenza worked as a Senior Project Manager for SHoP Construction in 2013 and has since transitioned to a position at Forest City Ratner Companies. As a Senior Vice President in the Design and Construction group, Alexis manages in house projects, and is currently running the renovation of the Nassau Coliseum.

Frank Lettieri is currently retired from full-time work, but is still employed in a per diem position as a Hemodialysis Nurse. Hurricane Sandy was the chief reason for his retiring. Spiritual matters, the lives of his five children, the upcoming birth of his first grandchild, and his wife's imminent retirement are his main interests.

Suzanne Lettieri was the Project Leader for *Party Wall* and a Visiting Critic at Cornell University. She is currently a Michigan-Mellon Design Fellow and Co-Principal of Je-Le.

Jessica Levine received an M.Arch from Cornell in 2013. Originally from Toronto, she is currently working in New York City.

Mikey Loverich was squatting in various apartments in New York City in 2013. Now he squats various houses in Philadelphia and on an island in Puget Sound.

James Lowder teaches at the Irwin S. Chanin School of Architecture at the Cooper Union and at Cornell University. He is a founding partner at LMNOP.

Chet McPhatter is Chief Operating Office of Banker Steel, based in Lynchburg, Virginia. Among their high-profile art-based projects, they recently completed the Whitney Museum in New York City.

Martin Miller has taught at Cornell University since Fall 2013, and is design director and founder of Antistatics.

Chris Mills is the Managing Member of Hydro Composites, LLC, a custom fiberglass fabrication company in Stockdale, Texas. He is now also the Managing Member of LMM Properties, LLC, and a sitting Board Member of Mills Farm, LLC.

Pauline Morrow is Caroline's Mother. She lives in Derry, Northern Ireland, and is working on her autobiography. She got a commendation in her exams and received an award for outstanding personal achievement.

Mike Moyer served as Assistant Dean of Alumni Affairs and Development at the College of Architecture Art and Planning from 2007 through 2013. He is now Associate Vice President of Development for Colleges at Virginia Tech University.

Richard Nelson-Chow was a student at Cornell AAP in 2013. He is currently a junior architect at OMA New York.

Zachary Tyler Newton was a freelance architectural designer in 2013. Today, he additionally practices architectural photography, as well as exhibition design and planning for a major artist.

Sarah Obraitis is co-owner of M. Wells Dinette at MoMA PS1, as well as the M. Wells Steakhouse.

William O'Brien Jr., Principal of WOJR: Organization for Architecture, is Associate Professor in the MIT Department of Architecture and a co-founder of Collective–LOK.

Caroline O'Donnell is Principal of CODA, Edgar A. Tafel Associate Professor of Architecture at Cornell University, and Editor-in-Chief of the Cornell Journal of Architecture. Since 2013, she has written her first book, *Niche Tactics*, and worked on several new pavilions, including *Urchin*, a pavilion made of chairs, as well as some less temporary designs.

Fergal O'Donnell was Director of Service Delivery at T-Systems North America, in 2013. He is currently Head of Quality at T-Systems North America. He has climbed four of the 'Seven Summits' peaks, and he lives in Frisco, Texas with his wife, Joanna, and daughter, Tara. He is working on his first novel, *Proconnesus*.

Tara O'Donnell was the winner of Food Network's *Chopped Junior* cooking show in 2016 and she has since started her own catering company. She is currently in eighth grade.

Juanito Olivarria is a 3D artist, composer, and founder of Luxigon. He is currently based out of Los Angeles, California.

Nat Oppenheimer is a structural engineer in New York City. In 2013 he was, and still is, a Principal and Executive Vice President at Silman.

Giffen Clark Ott earned his B.Arch from Cornell University in 2013. He runs a store in San Francisco, a gallery in Oakland, and continues to make things and figure it all out.

Gosia Pawlowska was a second-year B.Arch student at Cornell in 2013. After graduating with a thesis project made of sugar, she is currently an aspiring architect based in New York City.

Ryan Paxton was not just the lighting guy for SFDS in 2013. He is currently a freelance digital fabricator and designer based in Brooklyn, New York, and founding member of LensCloud, a company that produces 3D scanning devices.

Shane Pickles is the husband of Caroline's sister, Paula, and father of Milly and Christopher. He is now an armorer with the New Zealand Air Force.

Joe Raia, the inventor of Softrucks, continues to build the Softrucks brand while running Garage Manufacturing, a product development company in New York.

Florencia Rausch was teaching at University Torcuato Di Tella in Buenos Aires in 2013, as well as being a partner at GRMR Architects, where she continues today.

Susan T. Rodriguez is a founding partner of Ennead Architects (formerly Polshek Partnership). She now runs an independent practice in New York City. Her work focuses on the intersection of architecture and the public realm. She has served on the Cornell University Board of Trustees, the Dean's Advisory Council of the College of Architecture, Art and Planning, as well as the boards of the Architectural League of New York and Art Works Projects: For Human Rights.

Bryan Roe is President and CEO of Koolfog, based in Palm Desert, California.

David Rosas is the Logistics Manager for Design Miami, a collectible design fair that runs concurrently with Art Basel in Miami and Switzerland. In 2013, he was a project manager for a production company in charge of projects like Univision and Telemundo's award shows, Art Basel, and events such as the Ultra Music Festival.

Jason Salfi is co-founder of Comet Skateboards.

David Salomon is Assistant Professor and Co-ordinator of the Architectural Studies Program at Ithaca College.

Yeung Shin was a Teaching Associate for the first-year B.Arch studio at Cornell in 2013. She is currently working as a freelance designer in Seoul.

Andrea Simitch was Associate Professor in the Department of Architecture at Cornell University, as well as being a partner in Simitch + Warke Architecture. She is now Department Chair.

John Sinnott manages the Industrial Partnerships Program at the Cornell Center for Materials Research; fostering economic development and knowledge transfer to small businesses in New York State.

Meinolf Schulte was the managing director of Krinner Canada in 2013. The company name has since changed to Bayo.S Canada, and Meinolf is now president/owner.

Mei-Lan Tan was known as Rachel Tan, a fourth-year B.Arch student, in 2013. She graduated in 2016 and is now producing her own small objects as UMÉ Studio.

Peter Turner was AAP's Assistant Dean, Administration during a decade of change where $100 million of facility improvements repositioned the college for the future. He retired in 2015.

Richard Wilson was and is Chief of Installation at MoMA PS1.

Eric J. Winston was Director at SFDS LLC in 2013. He is currently Director at SFDS LLC, and also Principal at 32 Square and Boneyard Pets.

John Zissovici was and still is Associate Professor at Cornell University, equally interested in the material and immaterial aspects of architecture.

Credits: Party Wall *at MoMA PS1*

Steel erection: JC Steel · *Steel fabrication:* Banker Steel · *Steel:* Metals USA · *Production management:* SFDS · *Pool decks:* Component Assembly Systems · *Bladders:* Extra-Packaging · *Bench legs:* Emeco · *Bench pads:* Softrucks · *Water consultation:* Fluidity Design · *Layout:* Langan · *Pools:* Hydro-Composites · *Mister:* Koolfog · *Foundation:* Krinner Screws · *Decks:* Olollo · *T-shirts:* American Apparel · *Transport:* Lynchburg Freight · *Bolts:* Weinstock Bros.

Thanks to:

Turner Construction, SHoP Construction, Ryan Paxton, HWKN, MOS

Special thanks to:

Philip Eisenberg, Jody Gorton, Dan Kaplan, FAIA, and Amy Graydon, Elise Jaffe + Jeffrey Brown, Mr. & Mrs. L. P. Kwee, Alison Levasseur, Helene Lindenfeld, Gene and Pamela McGuire, Jon & Nancy Pundyk, Celeste Robbins, Susan Rodriguez, Paul Rubacha, Renee Dake Wilson

And especially:

Kent Kleinman and Cornell University, College of Architecture, Art, and Planning, and Department of Architecture; and Cornell Center for Materials Research

Consultants for Competition Phase:

Structural Engineer: Silman Associates (Nat Oppenheimer, Scott Hughes, Paul Laroque) · *Water:* Fluidity Design (Jim Garland) · *Water Ballast:* Interstate Products (Scott Sagalow) · *Scaffolding Engineer:* Plan B Engineering (John McErlean) · *Mechanical Engineer:* Buro Happold (Jeff Thompson, Chris Coulter) · *Facade:* Werner Sobek (Chris Johnson) · *Fashion:* American Apparel (Iris Alonzo) · *Media:* 2x4 (Georgianna Stout)

CODA

Design Team, Ithaca, NY:

Caroline O'Donnell (Principal), Suzanne Lettieri (Team Leader), Stephen Clipp, Michael Jefferson, Jessica Tranquada, with:

Construction Team, Queens, NY:

William (Trey) Anderson, Nils Axen, Mike Babcock, Vivian Chen, Joon Choe, Ryland Dandretta, Ryan Drummond, Ben Hoffman, Bari Felix, Nathan Friedman, John Lai, Varya Larionova, Spencer Lapp, Roger Mainor, Ashley Mendelsohn, Richard Nelson-Chow, Fergal O'Donnell, Shane Pickles, Ashley Reed, Stephen Max Silverstein

Skateboard Saturday Team, Ithaca, NY:
Jordan Berta, Nicholas Cassab-Gheta, Andrew Fu, Andrew Hart, Ben Kessler, Siobhan Lee, David Salomon, Olivia Salomon, Heriberto Rodriguez, Daniel Toretsky

Competition Team, Ithaca, NY:
Nathan Friedman, Lucas Greco, Noah Ives, Joseph Kennedy, Jerry Lai, Jessica Levine, Juanito Olivarria, Chris Ray, Daniel Salomon, Yeung Shin, Rachel Tan

Cornell University, Ithaca NY:
Mark Cruvellier, Tom Frank, Andre Hafner, Rich Jaenson, Kent Kleinman, Mike Moyer, Frank Parish, Andrea Simitch, Melinda Stelick, Margaret Timmons, Peter Turner, Steve Yaros

Thanks also to:
Jason Anderson, Sarah Arfaian, Austin Beierle, Charles Burke, Patrick Delahoy, Richie Jolta, Viola Kosseda, Jackie Krasnokutskaya, James Lowder, Le Luo, Jennifer Mayfield, Dan Marino, Isidoro Michan, Isabel Oyuel-Bonzani, Gosia Pawlowska, Tony-Saba Shiber, Elizabeth Suarez, Catherine Witt

Image credits

I · The Competition

American Apparel: 63
CODA: 16, 18-19, 22, 23, 24, 26, 27, 28, 30, 36–37, 39, 40, 48, 54-55, 57, 59, 64, 67, 70, 73, 82, 84, 90, 91
CODA with Fluidity: 79
Comet Skateboards: 53
Kevin Hagen/NYDN: 25
Eduard Hueber: 60
Juanito Olivarria: 75, 76-77
Red Antler: 51

II · The Design Development

CODA: 98, 103, 108, 110, 112, 113, 115, 121, 122, 129, 133
DataDraft: 136-137
Suzanne Lettieri: 118
Zachary Tyler Newton: 130

III · The Install

CODA: 149, 150, 154-155, 161, 163, 167, 176, 181, 183, 190, 191, 194, 197
Zachary Tyler Newton: 152, 158, 160, 166, 173, 177, 182, 185, 189

IV · The Wall

Jason Anderson: 216
CODA: 210, 212, 235, 262
Cornell: 223
Luciana Golcman/Time Out: 221
Zachary Tyler Newton: 206, 207, 209, 218-219, 224, 228, 236, 238-239, 246-247, 254, 258-259, 266-267
Florencia Rausch: 252

Cover: Andrea Simitch

Name index

**underlined pages denote authors of text*

Acknowledgments

Thanks to Jose Ibarra, Martin Miller, Kent Kleinman, Elise Gold, Sarah Walsh, Melissa Constantine, and the College of Architecture, Art, and Planning at Cornell.

Special thanks to all of our contributors and to everyone who participated in the *Party Wall* project. While our credit list is long, there are inevitably many who were involved who are not listed.

This is Not a Wall

Collected Short Stories
on CODA's *Party Wall*
at MoMA PS1

Published by Cornell AAP
Publications

Editors: Caroline O'Donnell &
Steven Chodoriwsky
Design: Steven Chodoriwsky
Printing: Thomson-Shore Inc
Cover image: Andrea Simitch

ISBN-10: 0-9972602-0-3
ISBN-13: 978-0-9972602-0-5

Printed in USA

Distribution: Actar D, Inc.

New York
440 Park Avenue, 17th Floor
New York, NY 10016
Phone +1 212 966 2207
salesnewyork@actar-d.com

Barcelona
Roca i Batlle 2
08023 Barcelona, SP
T +34 933 282 183
eurosales@actar-d.com

$29.95 Worldwide